HISTORY • PLAYERS • TOURNAMENTS • FOLKLORE • MYTHS • TRIVIA

So, You Think You Know TENNIS?

Published by Omni Publishing Co.

www.omni-pub.com

Library of Congress cataloging in publication data:

Quinlan, Henry M.

So, You Think You Know Tennis?

History, Players, Tournaments, Folklore, Myths, Trivia

First Printing Edition 2023

ISBN: 978-1-928758-07

So, You Think You Know TENNIS?

HISTORY
PLAYERS
TOURNAMENTS
FOLKLORE
MYTHS
TRIVIA

HENRY M. QUINLAN

"To err is human. To put the blame on someone else is doubles."—ANONYMOUS

Dedication

I am dedicating this book to my friend, Tom Larkin, a friend for 60 plus years. After we left Boston College, he went into the Marines, and I went into the Army and then we took different paths. Twenty years ago, we reconnected serendipitously at a tennis court and have played many times since. Tom was a standout player who had many titles, and was a certified teaching pro. I always thought his tennis skills were first developed during his days as a Golden Glove boxing champion.

Tom was a kind, good friend who possessed a wonderful sense of humor and his memory contained an unlimited number of Irish jokes. Anyone who ever met him or played against him never forgot this smiling, good man. I want to thank his wife Ann and children, Susan, Carolyn and Thomas for sharing Tom with the rest of us. He was a treasure.

"The one thing you can never forget: The game will live on. It does not matter who is the World's No. 1, or who was the best, or who will be the best. The game is bigger than everybody."— ROGER FEDERER

Introduction

My goal with this book is to broaden the knowledge of tennis players everywhere about the history, the players, the rules, and its unique unspoken sportsmanship traditions. I believe when tennis players have a greater knowledge about the game there comes a greater appreciation. When I watch the great men's players of today, I remember watching Jack Kramer play before 3000 people at Boston Garden and marvel at how the game has developed. When I see the great women players today I appreciate even more the stand the "Original 9" took when they made their victorious statement so many years ago.

I have watched some of the greatest players in the history of the game play and I can appreciate their talent and drive. But I have also watched just average players play with every bit of enthusiasm that they can muster just to compete. Seeing a player at any level giving one hundred per cent effort is always a special treat.

The players, the equipment, the training have all gotten much better. But the players, at all levels, still enjoy playing the game no matter where they play—in Arthur Ashe Stadium or some obscure court that will remain unknown to 99.9% of tennis players.

I just want to share my love for this game with all readers and to wish them good luck whenever they play this wonderful game.

So, You Think You Know Tennis?

Contents

"Tennis isn't about getting somewhere; it's about enjoying the experience and learning the lessons it teaches you.—ARTHUR ASHE

Preface

I love tennis. I first picked up a racket in 1947 at Dean Playground in Brookline, Massachusetts. Now, 76 years later, I am still playing and still loving the game. It has given me great friends, special relationships with my grandchildren, and wonderful memories playing tennis on courts both in the U.S. and in different countries. The health benefits, both mental and physical, are self-evident to me.

I ♥ TENNIS

I have been a winner and a loser—though winning is better. No matter the score, I am good. I am playing the game I love.

I played little between the ages of 16 and 41. Then I started to play with my old high school friend Dan Shea, who was also the high school tennis coach. The night after my first match with him I landed in the hospital with severe cramps—because I was using long-neglected muscles. For the next 20 years, I played with Dan. Then another friend, Dick Elia, joined us, and we played at least once a week. To this day I continue to play.

I have had many interesting and memorable experiences playing tennis, starting in my youthful days.

The Longwood Cricket Club is in Brookline, Massachusetts. Once a year young players from the public playgrounds of Brookline were invited to visit and play with the club's young players. On my first trip to Longwood at age 10, what I remember most was seeing tennis balls everywhere on all the courts. I had never seen so many tennis balls all in one place. I was coming from a place where a new ball was a rare event. Having three new balls at the same time was unheard of. I remember thinking, Wow, I never saw so many tennis balls in my life—and none are bald.

Henry Quinlan and Yevgeny Zimin

I still remember my first match. I was in my usual long brown pants with brown sneakers and my opponent, a member, appeared in an all-white ensemble of shirt, shorts and tennis shoes. I won the match but the whole time I was thinking how can I take some of these balls home? I skipped the next round and instead a friend and I loaded up as many balls as we could carry and left the club with big smiles. Years later when I played, as a guest, on the beautiful grass courts, my first thought of entering the club was the remembrance of my first visit.

I lived in Moscow in the early nineties and played a lot of tennis, primarily with Yevgeny Zimin, one of the greatest hockey players in the history of the USSR. He had three Olympic Gold Medals and four World Hockey Championships. Wherever we played in Moscow there was always a small crowd present to watch...him.

One day a businessperson invited me to play at a court in his office building in downtown Moscow. When I got there, I was surprised to see a full-size court that had only four feet between the baselines and a wall. The sidelines of the court had a wall on one side and windows on the other, both only two feet away. I soon discovered "home court advantage" really meant something.

After Moscow I lived in Brooklyn and played tennis at the courts in Prospect Park. There were ten clay courts. In the winter they were covered with a tent. There were a lot of particularly good

The Mattapoisett Players—Lou Roy, Bill Short, Wayne Miller, and Henry Quinlan

players, among them a stereotypical, aggressive New Yorker. He loved to challenge calls on my base line—while he was standing behind his own baseline. I enjoyed the competition.

My favorite court is in Brooklyn. It is a lone court below Brooklyn Heights. From one side of the court there is a clear view of lower Manhattan. It is a spectacular sight.

After Brooklyn, I moved to Wareham, Massachusetts where I played for many years in Mattapoisett and Marion. There I enjoyed making good friends who were also skillful players. At that time, I was playing two to three times a week year-round. Good matches with good friends...the best.

One of the highlights for me was playing with the group at the Newport Casino, home of the International Tennis Hall of Fame. I remember being shocked at the size of the men's locker room—only the size of a big double closet. I wondered how that worked

Two of my challenging opponents— Jill Mansfield of Nashua, NH and John Clifford, Wareham MA

during a tournament. My son, Tom's company won a contract to paint the casino buildings and he inserted into the contract two tickets for me to attend Pete's Sampras' induction into the Hall of Fame.

While living in Wareham, I introduced my six grandchildren to the game. They all know how to play now and two played in high school. One granddaughter was lured away by her success in soccer, while her sister played tennis for four years and was captain in her senior year. Many hours well spent.

I spent three months in Aix-en-Provence in the south of France. A club there granted me free access to their courts. I joined with other members who were seniors like me, and we played mixed doubles. During one match I was partnered with an attractive lady from Paris, an exceptionally good player who had a vacation

Grandchildren — Kelly Quinlan, Emily Murphy, Caroline Murphy, and Ryan Quinlan

Tennis group in Aix en Provance, France

home in Aix. During one changeover she said to me, "I need five minutes," and I responded, "Why?" She quickly replied, "I need to fix my make-up." A true Parisian lady.

For the past two years I have been living in Merrimack, New Hampshire. I have been playing at the Longfellow New Hampshire Tennis and Swim Club in Nashua. As it has been doing all my life, tennis has led me to find new friends, and I continue to play a lot of tennis year-round. Every Saturday my friends and I play two and a half hours of competitive tennis. We play with both men and women.

The game of tennis has given me so much. I am a proud advocate for the game. I hope this book deepens your knowledge of the sport as well as giving you a greater appreciation and love for the game.

The Nashua Players: Robert Gamache, Melissa Salmon, Roy Hugenberger, Henry Quinlan

History of Tennis

The term "tennis" is thought to derive from the French word tenez, which means "take heed"—a warning from the server to the receiver.

Tennis originated in 12th century France, where it was played with the palm of the hand. The modern version of the game, played with rackets, emerged in the late 19th century. The first official tennis tournament, the All England Lawn Tennis and Croquet Club Championship, was held in 1877.

Tennis quickly gained popularity in Europe and the United States in the late 19th and early 20th centuries. The Davis Cup, the premier international team event in men's tennis, began in 1900, and the first women's tournament, the Wightman Cup, was held in 1923. The first professional tennis tour was established in 1926. The sport's governing body, the International Tennis Federation, was formed in 1913.

In the 1960s and 1970s, the sport experienced a major upheaval with the introduction of open tennis, allowing both amateur and professional players to compete together. This led to the formation of the ATP (Association of Tennis Professionals) for men and the WTA (Women's Tennis Association) for women. The game has continued to evolve with new technologies and training methods that have helped players to improve their performance.

Tennis has become a global sport, with millions of players and fans all over the world. The top players are well-known and highly paid athletes, and the Grand Slam tournaments are among the most watched and most lucrative sporting events in the world. Today, Tennis is widely played at amateur level as well as professional level with many tournaments and leagues held worldwide.

The four Grand Slam tournaments, which make up the most prestigious events in the sport, are the Australian Open, the French Open, Wimbledon, and the US Open. In addition to the Grand Slam tournaments, there are many other important events in the tennis calendar, including the ATP Tour and the WTA Tour. These are series of tournaments held throughout the year that culminate in the year-end ATP Tour Finals and the WTA Finals. These events feature the top players in the world competing for ranking points and prize money.

Tennis is also enjoyed at the grassroots level, with programs and initiatives in place to introduce the sport to children and young people around the world. Many countries have strong junior development programs, which help to identify and nurture the next generation of top players.

In recent years, the sport has also seen an increasing number of players from different backgrounds and cultures, breaking barriers and creating a more diverse representation in the sport. Sport continues to evolve and adapt, with new technologies and innovations being introduced to improve the game and make it more accessible to players and fans alike.

Real tennis—one of several games sometimes called "the sport of kings"—is the original racquet sport from which the modern game of tennis (also called "lawn tennis") is derived.

It is also known as court tennis in the United States, formerly royal tennis in England and Australia, and courte-paume in France (to distinguish it from longue-paume, and in reference to the older, racquetless game of jeu de paume, the ancestor of modern handball and racquet games). Many French real tennis courts are at jeu de paume clubs.

Real tennis evolved, over three centuries, from an earlier ball game played around the 12th century in France. This had some similarities to palla, fives, Spanish pelota or handball, in that it involved hitting a ball with a bare hand and later with a glove. By the 16th century, the glove had become a racquet, the game had moved to an enclosed playing area, and the rules had stabilized. Real tennis spread across Europe, with the Papal Legate reporting in 1596.

The term real was first used by journalists in the early 20th century as a retronym to distinguish the ancient game from modern lawn tennis.

Indoor Tennis Court

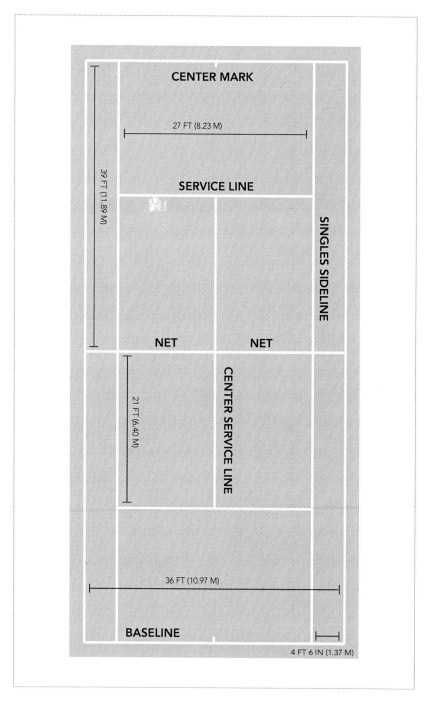

The Tennis Court

The first official tennis court was built in 1875 in Birmingham, England. The modern game of tennis, with its current scoring system and rules, was established in the late 19th century. There are four main types of surfaces for tennis courts: Grass, clay, hard and artificial grass.

In total, tennis courts measure 78ft x 36ft or 2,808 square feet. However, the full area of the court is used only for doubles matches. The singles court measures 78ft x 27ft or 2,106 square feet. Every court is composed of quite a few elements, here are each component.

The service line runs parallel to the net and marks the halfway point between the net and the baseline. It also marks the end of the service boxes. It is 27ft in length. However, unlike the baseline, it extends only to the singles sidelines.

The baseline runs parallel to the net and defines the farthest boundary, or back of the court, on each side. 36ft for doubles, 27ft for singles.

The Center line is 4 inches in length.

The service line runs parallel to the net and marks the halfway point between the net and the baseline. It also marks the end of the service boxes. It is 27ft in length.

The center service line runs perpendicular to the net and meets the service line to create two equal-sized service boxes. It is 42ft long. 21ft on each side.

The Tennis Net

The tennis net is a barrier that divides the playing area of a tennis court in half, running parallel to the sidelines. It is typically made of nylon or other synthetic materials and is 3ft 6in. (1.07

meters) high at the center, tapering down to 3ft (0.91 meters) at the posts. The net is supported by a cord that runs through the top of the net and attaches to the posts, which are typically made of metal or composite materials. The purpose of the net is to make the game more challenging by forcing players to hit the ball over it to score points.

History of the Tennis Ball

The modern tennis ball can be traced back to the mid-19th century. The first tennis balls were made of cloth stuffed with feathers. These balls were quite different from the rubber balls used today, as they were much softer and less bouncy. In the 1870s, rubber was first used to create tennis balls, but they were not as widely adopted as the feather-filled balls. It wasn't until the 1920s that rubber balls began to replace feather-filled balls in sport. The first pressurized tennis balls were introduced in the 1940s, which allowed for better consistency and performance on the court. Today, most tennis balls are made of rubber and are pressurized with air or nitrogen.

Originally, tennis balls were white, now they are mostly yellow.

The Tennis Racquet

The history of the tennis racquet dates back to the 12th century, when a crude version of the game was played with the hand. The racket as we know it today was not invented until the 16th century. The first racket was made of wood and had a handle with strings stretched across the frame. Over time, the material used to make rackets has evolved from wood to metal, and now to modern materials such as graphite and carbon fiber. The size, shape, and weight of the racket have also changed over the years to suit different playing styles and preferences. Today, tennis rackets are highly advanced, with sophisticated designs and materials that offer players greater control, power, and precision.

Scoring—History

The origins of the 15, 30, and 40 scores are believed to be medieval French. The earliest reference is in a ballad by Charles D'Orleans in 1435 which refers to quarante cirq ("forty-five"), which gave rise to modern 40. In 1522, there is a sentence in Latin "we are winning 30, we are winning 45". The first recorded theories about the origin of 15 were published in 1555 and 1579. However, the origins of this convention remain obscure.

It is sometimes believed that clock faces were used to keep score on court, with a quarter move of the minute hand to indicate a score of 15, 30, and 45. When the hand moved to 60, the game was over. However, in order to ensure that the game could not be won by a one-point difference in players' scores, the idea of "deuce" was introduced. To make the score stay within the "60" ticks on the clock face, the 45 was changed to 40. Therefore, if both players had 40, the first player to score would receive ten, and that would move the clock to 50. If the player scored a second time before the opponent is able to score, they would be awarded another ten and the clock would move to 60. The 60 signifies the end of the game. However, if a player fails to score twice in a row, then the clock would move back to 40 to establish another "deuce".[4][5]

Although this suggestion might sound attractive, the first reference to tennis scoring (as mentioned above) is in the 15th century, and at that time clocks measured only the hours (1 to 12). It was not until about 1690, when the more accurate pendulum escapement was invented, that clocks regularly had minute hands. So the concept of tennis scores originating from the clock face could not have come from medieval times.[6]

However, the clock at Wells Cathedral in England which dates from 1386 had an inner dial with 60 minutes and a minute indicator and tolled every quarter hour. Likewise the clock erected at Rouen, France, in 1389 tolled every fifteen minutes. So by the end of the 14th century, on the most advanced clocks, minutes were being marked and quarter hours were being tolled. So a clock face with minutes and quarter hours would likely have been familiar to the English and French nobles by 1435 and 1522. It is not hard to imagine that they might use a mockup of a clock face to keep score and that they would score by quarter hours since that is when the clocks tolled.[7][8]

The use of "love" for zero probably derives from the phrase "playing for love", meaning "without stakes being wagered, for nothing". Another explanation is that it derives from the French expression for "the egg" (l'œuf) because an egg looks like the number zero. This is similar to the origin of the term "duck" in cricket, supposedly from "duck's egg", referring to a batsman who has been called out without scoring a run. Another possibility comes from the Dutch expression "iets voor lof doen", which means to do something for praise, implying no monetary stakes. Another theory on the origins of the use of "love" comes from the notion that, at the start of any match, when scores are at zero, players still have "love for each other".

Game Scoring

In standard play, scoring beyond a "deuce" score, in which the players have scored three points each, requires that one player must get two points ahead in order to win the game. This type of tennis scoring is known as "advantage scoring" (or "ads"). The side which wins the next point after deuce is said to have the advantage. If they lose the next point, the score is again deuce, since the score is tied. If the side with the advantage wins the next point, that side has won the game, since they have a lead of two points. When the server is the player with the advantage, the score may be called as "advantage in". When the server's opponent has the advantage, the score may be called "advantage out". These phrases are sometimes shortened to "ad in" or "van in" (or "my ad") and "ad out" (or "your ad"). Alternatively, the players' names are used: in professional tournaments the umpire announces the score in this format (e.g., "advantage Nadal" or "advantage Williams").

In the USTA rule book (but not the ITF rules), there is the following comment: "'Zero,' 'one,' 'two,' and 'three,' may be substituted for 'Love', '15', '30', and '40.' This is particularly appropriate for matches with an inexperienced player or in which one player does not understand English."

Set Scoring

In tennis, a set consists of a sequence of games played with alternating service and return roles. There are two types of set formats that require different types of scoring.

An advantage set is played until a player or team has won at least six games and that player or team has a two-game lead over their opponent(s). The set continues, without tiebreak(er), until a player or team wins the set by two games. Advantage sets are no longer played under the rules of the USTA. nor in the Australian Open starting from 2019; and since 2022 for all other tournaments, including the French Open, Fed Cup & the Olympics. Wimbledon, from 2019 to 2021, used a unique scoring system for the last set where the players continued to play after 6–all as in an advantage set until a player earned a two-game lead.

However, if the players reached 12–all, a seven-point tie-breaker was played to determine the winner. Mixed doubles at the Grand

Slams (except for Wimbledon) are a best-of-three format with the final set being played as a "Super Tie Break" (sometimes referred to as a "best-of-two" format) even at Wimbledon, which still plays a best-of-three match with all sets played as tie-break sets.

Check all Standard Tie-breaks.

A tie-break set is played with the same rules as the advantage set, except that when the score is tied at 6–6, a tie-break game (or tiebreaker) is played. Typically, the tie-break game continues until one side has won seven points with a margin of two or more points. However, many tie-break games are played with different tiebreak point requirements, such as eight or 10 points. Often, a seven-point tie-breaker is played when the set score is tied at 6–6 to determine who wins the set. If the tiebreak score gets to 6–6, then whichever player to win the best of two points wins the set.

People of Significance

The modern game of tennis was created in the late 19th century by two Englishmen named Major Walter Clopton Wingfield and Harry Gem. Major Wingfield is credited with devising the original rules of the game in 1873, which he called 'sphairistike'. His prototype set used a rectangular court, an hourglass-shaped net, and a rubber ball.

Harry Gem was an avid tennis player and was exposed to the sport while studying law at Oxford University. In 1872, he partnered with Augurio Perera to create a modified version of lawn tennis. The two men used a larger court size that measured 66ft by 26ft—the standard size of today's tennis courts—and introduced gutta-percha balls for play. The net post height was also raised from three feet to nearly four and a half feet tall. Augurio

Perera, also introduced a new technique for striking balls with a racquet. Perera left England three years after Gem's death in 1881, and his life after this date is unknown.

In addition to these modifications, Wingfield and Gem are credited with developing the basic scoring system used today in tennis. This includes 15, 30, 40 and game points as well as love (zero) points. They also added gameplay elements such as volleys, foot faults, double faults, service court boundaries and out-of-boundary shots during play.

By 1874, Wingfield had successfully marketed his version of sphairistike as "Lawn Tennis" throughout Europe leading to its popularization across England and beyond. Although it wasn't until 1877 that the Marylebone Cricket Club officially recognized Lawn Tennis with their own detailed set of rules for play —which remain largely unchanged to this day.

Nowadays professional tournaments such as Wimbledon take place annually attracting both players from all over the world along with thousands of spectators who come to watch one of the most beloved sports on earth—all thanks to this dynamic duo who helped create it!

Other men who also played an instrumental role in helping develop modern-day tennis include; William Renshaw and Ernest Renshaw, two brothers from England who popularized doubles play; French engineer Jean Jaques Perrottet who invented the first cork-centered tennis ball; German physicist August Dettweiler who designed grapite-fiber reinforced rackets which revolutionized power play; and more recently used by former professional player Rod Laver who won 11 Grand Slam singles titles between 1960 and 1969—helping cement him as one of the greatest players ever seen.

DO YOU KNOW?

History of Tennis

- The rules of modern tennis have changed little since the 1890s. Two exceptions are that until 1961 the server had to keep one foot on the ground at all times, and the adoption of the tiebreak in the 1970s.

- The invention of the first lawn mower in Britain in 1830 is believed to have been a catalyst for the preparation of modern-style grass courts, sporting ovals, playing fields, pitches, greens, etc. This in turn led to the codification of modern rules for many sports, including lawn tennis, most football codes, lawn bowls and others.

- "Tennis balles" are mentioned by William Shakespeare in his play Henry V (1599), when a basket of them is given to King Henry as a mockery of his youth and playfulness.

- The term "love" used to describe a score of zero comes from the French word "l'oeuf" which means "egg" and was used because a zero looks like an egg.

- Stadium or tournament courts have an additional 10 ft on both the length and width of the overall dimensions of the court are suggested to give extra perimeter area for judges to stand and for player overrun. Therefore, the overall court length would be 130 ft and overall width would be 70 ft

- Break back means to win a game as the receiving player or team immediately after losing the previous game as the serving player or team.

- English King Henry VIII built a tennis court at Hampton Court Palace. While this exact court is no longer in existence, a similar court was built in its place in 1625. It is still in use today.

- Breadstick is a colloquial term for winning or losing a set 6–1, with the straight shape of the one supcosedly being reminiscent of the straight shape of a breadstick.

- Tthe first rackets used for playing tennis were made of wood and strung with pig-gut.

- Tennis rackets were made of wood between the 15th century and 1965.

- The first steel racquet was built by Rene LaCoste a French tennis player. It caused tennis rackets to have larger heads and to string at a higher tension.

- Jimmy Connors was the first professional tennis player to use a steel tennis racket because it provided more power.

- The vast majority of tennis rackets are manufactured in Asia with Japan being the leading producer.

- The first-time tennis shorts were worn in a major tournament was 1932 when Henry "Bunny" Austin wore shorts at Wimbledon.

- Bill Tilden was also a fashion trend setter. His style of wearing a long sleeve shirt with the arms rolled up to the elbow was a fashion trend in the 1930's.

*Many consider Novak
Djokovic the greatest men's
player of all time. And that
will be the case until the
next GOAT comes along.*

The Greatest Men Tennis Players

and Millions More

PARIS, FRANCE—MAY 31, 2022: Grand Slam champion Novak Djokovic of Serbia in action during his quarter-final match against Rafael Nadal of Spain at 2022 Roland Garros in Paris, France.

NOVAK DJOKOVIC

Novak Djokovic is a Serbian professional tennis player who has earned the nickname of "The Joker" for his humorous and entertaining on-court manner. He has been one of the most successful players in the professional circuit over the past decade, holding an impressive 23 Grand Slam titles and a record 38 ATP Masters titles. Djokovic has also achieved an historic feat by winning all four Grand Slams consecutively from 2015 to 2016, something that had never been done before in the Open Era.

Djokovic's success is built upon an outstanding serve and court coverage that makes him one of the toughest opponents around. His endurance and adaptability have made him a formidable force in major tournaments, where he routinely reaches deep into rounds and finals. His successes have helped him become only the second male player to reach seven hundred career wins since Lleyton Hewitt in 2019.

He holds multiple records such as most consecutive weeks at number one (122), most consecutive wins on hard courts (33) and becoming only the sixth man ever to complete a career Grand Slam.

"In terms of playing ability there is nothing to choose between number one and 100. Instead, it's a question of who believes and who wants it more? Which player is mentally stronger? Which player is going to fight the hardest in the big points? These are the things that determine who is the champion." Novak Djokovic.

DO YOU KNOW?

Novak Djokovic

◆ Representing Serbia, Djokovic led the Serbian national team to their first Davis Cup title in 2010 and to the inaugural ATP Cup title in 2020.

◆ The Novak Djokovic Foundation partnered with the World Bank in August 2015 to promote early childhood education in Serbia. His foundation has built fifty schools as of April 2022 and are building their 51st and supported more than 20,800 children and over a thousand families.

◆ On turning professional in 2003, Djokovic began wearing Adidas clothing. At the end of 2009, Djokovic signed a 10-year deal with the Italian clothing company Sergio Tacchini after Adidas refused to extend his clothing contract, choosing instead to sign Andy Murray.

◆ Djokovic has been reported to meditate for up to an hour a day at the Buddhist Buddhapadipa Temple in Wimbledon as he appreciates the natural setting and serenity, and is close to monks in the complex He has spoken of the positive power of meditation.

◆ In 1993, Djokovic was spotted by Yugoslav tennis player Jelena Gencic. She complimented the 6-year-old Djokovic as the greatest talent she ever saw since Monika Seles. She trained him for the next 6 years. When he was 13, he went to the Pilic Academy in Munich, Germany, to pursue higher levels of competition and when he was 14, he began his international career.

ROGER FEDERER

Roger Federer is a legendary professional tennis player whose career has spanned over two decades. He has won a record 20 Grand Slam titles, including eight Wimbledon Championships, six Australian Opens, five US Opens and one French Open. He is the first male player to win all four major singles tournaments at least five times each. He also holds the record for most ATP Tour wins with 103 and consecutive weeks at number one with 310 weeks.

Throughout his career, Federer has been recognized as one of the greatest players in history due to his success on the court. He was chosen as the world's best male tennis player by the Association of Tennis Professionals (ATP) for a record eight consecutive years from 2004 to 2012. In addition to this honor, Federer also earned numerous other awards and accolades, such as being named Laureus Sportsman of the Year in 2004 and 2005 and receiving an honorary knighthood from Queen Elizabeth II in 2009 for his services to tennis.

Federer's impact on tennis goes beyond just winning titles and awards; he is credited with introducing a new style of play that focuses on athleticism, precision, and control rather than aggressive power serves and groundstrokes. His attacking game-style has been adopted by many fellow players throughout the years, making him an innovator in the sport. Additionally, Federer has become a role model for aspiring athletes due to his commitment to integrity within the game and positive attitude towards fellow competitors.

DO YOU KNOW?

Roger Federer

◆ Aside from his extraordinary talent at tennis, Federer is also renowned for his powerful serves and work ethic on court; he is known as "The Maestro" for his court awareness, footwork, and shot making skills.

◆ He is also noted for his polite demeanor and well-spoken nature off court—in 2015, he was appointed as Goodwill Ambassador for UNICEF Switzerland which saw him raise funds to build schools in Africa.

◆ Few people know about Federer's nickname: "Fedex". It refers to how consistent he is—just like the company FedEx® ensures safe delivery of packages without fail! tennis player from Switzerland.

◆ Federer has devoted himself to philanthropy work by founding The Roger Federer Foundation which focuses on education projects throughout Africa and Switzerland.

◆ Federer started playing tennis when he was 8 years old, although at the time he also dabbled in other sports such as badminton and basketball. By the time he was 11 years old he was already the top junior tennis player. After this outstanding year, Federer decided to focus all of his athletic effort on tennis.

◆ As a serious teen player, Federer participated in 2 tournaments per month, traveling with his parents to different cities in order to compete with the best players in his league.

RAFAEL NADAL

Rafael Nadal is one of the most successful tennis players of all time, having won 22 Grand Slam titles and 14 French Open titles. He has also been ranked number one in the world several times, including a record-breaking 209 weeks at the top of the rankings.

Nadal's career began in 2001 when he turned professional at age 15. Since then, he has won numerous titles and awards, including winning every major event at least twice and becoming the first man to achieve a career Grand Slam on clay courts. His most notable achievements include winning a record 12 French Open championships, two US Opens, three Wimbledon Championships and two Australian Opens.

In addition to his success on the court, Nadal is known for his intense work ethic and never-give-up attitude that have earned him respect from fellow players and fans alike. He is also renowned for his strong ability to play defense with powerful groundstrokes that opponents find difficult to return. On top of this, Nadal has developed an extremely effective serve that can be used as both an offensive weapon and a defensive tool depending on the situation.

Overall, Rafael Nadal's tennis career is truly remarkable—having broken multiple records while inspiring many others with his drive and determination throughout his long professional journey.

Do You Know?

Rafael Nadal

◆ Rafael Nadal hits the heaviest topspin forehand in the game. His normal spin rate is 3,200 rpm and it has peaked at 5,000 rpm.

◆ Nadal has 81 consecutive wins on clay is the longest single-surface win streak in the Open Era.

◆ Nadal has won the Stefan Edberg Sportsmanship Award five times, and was the Laureus World Sportsman of the Year in 2011 and 2021. He is also a recipient of the Grand Cross of the Order of Dos De Mayo, the Grand Cross of Naval Merit, and the Medal of the City of Paris.

◆ When he was 14, the Spanish tennis federation requested that Nadal leave Mallorca and move to Barcelona to continue his tennis training. His family turned down this request, partly because they feared his education would suffer.

◆ In April 2014, he played the world's No. 1 female poker player, Vanessa Selbst, in a poker game in Monaco. In October 2020, Nadal competed in the professional-level Balearic Golf Championship, obtaining a World Amateur Golf Ranking in the process.

◆ Nadal's Uncle Tony might be well known for his coaching, but another uncle named Miguel Angel Nadal is a retired professional soccer player. He played for FC Barcelona and RCD Mallorca at the club level and even earned 62 caps with the Spanish national team.

PETE SAMPRAS

Peter Sampras is one of the most decorated tennis players in history, having won a total of 14 Grand Slam titles and 64 ATP Tour titles. He was the world number one ranked player for a record consecutive 286 weeks from 1993 to 1998 and held the record for most total weeks at number one until it was broken by Roger Federer in 2012. His career highlights include seven Wimbledon titles, five US Open championships, two Australian Opens, and a French Open title.

Sampras was renowned for his powerful serve which allowed him to hold onto points with ease and close out sets quickly. He also had strong return games and an all-around offensive play style that focused on aggression and power rather than finesse or strategy. As such, he often succeeded against opponents who were better tacticians or had better control over the court. He was feared by many opponents due to his mental strength and ability to stay focused during long rallies as well as his excellent composure when playing under pressure.

Off the court, Sampras is known for his humility, sportsmanship, and dedication to the game of tennis. He has been inducted into both the International Tennis Hall of Fame (2007) and the United States Olympic Hall of Fame (2009). roughout the years, making him an innovator in the sport. Additionally, Federer has become a role model for aspiring athletes due to his commitment to integrity within the game and positive attitude towards fellow competitors.

DO YOU KNOW?

Peter Sampras

◆ Sampras also gained notoriety for his mental strength and ability to remain cool under pressure during matches. He was known to never give up or throw in the towel when it looked like he could be defeated.

◆ From early on, his great idol was Rod Laver, and at the age of 11, Sampras met and played tennis with the legend.

◆ Sampras' 31-match Wimbledon win streak ended in a five set loss to Roger Federer, aged 19, in the fourth round; this was the only time the two tennis legends ever played an official professional match.

◆ In November 2010, Sampras reported that many of his trophies and memorabilia had been stolen from a West Los Angeles public storage facility. The loss included the trophy from his first Australian Open victory, two Davis Cups, an Olympic ring and six trophies for finishing top in the year-end rankings. Most of the stolen items have since been recovered and returned.

◆ Pete Sampras' elder sibling Stella, a late bloomer, had made her name coaching the women's tennis team UCLA. Tennis is also her passion; that is why she has decided to teach others how to be great at this game.

◆ The first person hired to Coach Pete Sampras tennis was Peter Fischer. Fischer's career was as a pediatrician, but he also had an interest in tennis. Training Pete was the first time Fischer has coached anyone to be a tennis player.

ROD LAVER

Rod Laver is one of the greatest tennis players of all time. He had an extraordinary career which spanned two decades from the mid-1950s to the late 1970s. He won a total of two hundred professional singles titles, including 11 Grand Slam titles and a record 22 Pro Slam tournaments.

Laver was one of the first players to take advantage of the newly introduced open era in 1968, allowing him to compete in both professional and amateur tournaments. His mastery on court was unparalleled, winning four consecutive Grand Slam titles (the Australian, French and US Opens plus Wimbledon). This feat has never been matched by any male tennis player in history and is thus known as 'The Grand Slam'.

He also reached remarkable heights during his doubles career with partner Ken Rosewall. The duo won thirteen major tournament titles together, most notably all four Grand Slam events in 1969–a feat that no other team has ever accomplished since then.

In addition to his success on court, Rod Laver was also widely recognized for his sportsmanship and humility off-court, which endeared him to fans around the world. He was inducted into the International Tennis Hall of Fame in 1981 and named Player of the Century by several publications over a decade later, cementing his legacy as one of the greatest athletes that have ever lived.

Do You Know?

Rod Laver

◆ Rod's mother was a world-famous opera singer from Richmond, Australia. She also loved playing tennis and was good at it. The family played tennis often. The two used to play tennis together. They, at one time, collaborated as a mother-son duo to play a junior event and they won the tournament.

◆ In 2000, the Centre Court Stadium at Melbourne Park, home of the Australian Open since 1988, was renamed Rod Laver Arena and a sculpture depicting him in action adorns the park grounds.

◆ In 1971 he became the first professional tennis player to surpass the $1,000,000 mark in career prize money, and he held on to his position as tennis's all-time leading money-winner until 1978.

◆ In 1976 the 38-year-old Laver retired from professional play, having won an unprecedented two hundred singles titles. However, he continued to compete at other levels, notably playing (1976–78) for the San Diego team of the World Team Tennis league.

◆ The Laver Cup tournament is an international hard court men's tennis tournament between Europe and the rest of the World that was founded in 2017. Roger Federer's management company, Jorge Paulo Lemann, Tennis Australia, and TEAM8 partnered to form the Laver Cup. It was intended to be the Ryder Cup of Tennis.

JIMMY CONNORS

James Scott Connors (born September 2, 1952) is an American former world No. 1 tennis player.

He started early at the age of 9 and began winning small tournaments. He is one of only nine players to win the Junior Orange Bowl twice. At 18 years of age in 1970, his first major victory came against Roy Emerson, another former world number 1. Two years later, he was playing professional tennis. He won the 1973 US Pro Singles title, against Arthur Ashe, his first major league title.

 He held the top Association of Tennis Professionals (ATP) ranking for a then-record 160 consecutive weeks from 1974 to 1977 and a career total of 268 weeks. Connors still holds three prominent Open Era men's singles records: 109 titles, 1,557 matches played, and 1,274 match wins.

His titles include eight major singles titles (a joint Open Era record five US Opens, two titles, one Australian Open), three year-end championships, and 17 Grand Prix Super Series titles. In 1974, he became the second man in the Open Era to win three major titles in a calendar year, and was not permitted to participate in the fourth, the French Open because of association with the World Team Tennis.. Connors finished year end number one in the ATP rankings from 1974 to 1978. In 1982, he won both Wimbledon and the US Open and was ATP Player of the Year and ITF World Champion. He retired in 1996 at the age of forty-three.

The tennis legend was inducted into the International Tennis Hall of Fame in 1998. He has a star on the St. Louis Walk of Fame.

DO YOU KNOW?

James Scott Connors

◆ During his best years of 1974 through 1978, Connors was challenged the most by Borg, with twelve matches on tour during that time limit. Borg won only four of those meetings, but two of those wins were in the Wimbledon finals of 1977 and 1978.

◆ In 1982, Connors experienced a resurgence as he defeated John McEnroe in five close sets to win Wimbledon and Ivan Lendl to win the US Open after which he reclaimed the ATP No. 1 ranking.

◆ In September 1992, Connors played Martina Navratilova in the third Battle of the Sexes tennis match at Caesars Palace in Las Vegas, Nevada. Connors was allowed only one serve per point and Navratilova was allowed to hit into half the doubles court. Connors won, 7–5, 6–2.

◆ Of his own competitive nature Connors has said, "There's always somebody out there who's willing to push it that extra inch, or mile, and that was me. (Laughter) I didn't care if it took me 30 minutes or five hours. If you beat me, you had to be the best, or the best you had that day. But that was my passion for the game. If I won, I won, and if I lost, well, I didn't take it so well."

◆ Jimmy Connors was never known to be a gentleman in the tennis world. His often more than rude demeanour earned him a lot of boos from the crowd. He even refused to participate in the 1977 all-stars parade.

THE REST OF THE BEST

All of the players listed below are among the greatest of all time, the first seven are subjective choices. Here those that complete the best of all time.

Stan Wawrinka, Guillermo Vilas, Jim Courier, Andy Murray, Ken Rosewall, Boris Becker, John Newcombe, Stan Edberg, Ivan Lendl, John McEnroe, Andre Agassi, Björn Borg. Each of these players are among the best ever to play the game.

Jimmy Connors and John McEnroe

Others to remember are Anthony Wilding, a New Zealander, arguably the first world champion and who was killed in World War I; Don Budge who was the first to win a calenda Grand Slam; Jack Kramer an American tennis player of the 1940s and 1950s. He won three Grand Slam tournaments. He led the U.S. Davis Cup tennis team to victory in the 1946 and 1947 Davis Cup finals. Kramer won the U.S. Pro Championship at Forest Hills in 1948 and the Wembley Pro Championships in 1949 Arthur Ashe was the first African American to win a Grand Slam event and he won two more. The main stadium where the US Open final is played is named after Arthur Ashe.

There are some players making a career with their tennis skills and some will emerge as champions supplanting those currently at the top. And then there are the rest of us.

Do You Know?

The Rest of Us

◆ Playing tennis is an incredibly enjoyable activity for amateur players. Not only does it provide a great way to stay fit and active, but it also provides a healthy outlet for competition and enjoyment. Tennis can be played as a social sport, allowing players to make new friends while enjoying the game, or it can be played as a solo sport, allowing players to hone their skills in a one-on-one atmosphere.

◆ Tennis is one of the most widely practiced sports in the world, with millions of people playing regularly. It has been proven to offer many mental and physical benefits, including improved coordination, better balance, increased strength and flexibility, improved stress management and relaxation, and more. Playing tennis helps players develop their strategic thinking and tactical skills; forcing them to constantly assess their opponents' strengths and weaknesses while adjusting their own strategies accordingly. This form of mental stimulation can result in greater focus in other areas of life such as work or school.

◆ The health benefits associated with playing tennis have been well documented; from reducing the risk of cardiovascular disease to improving bone strength due to regular impact with the ground during jumps and lunges. In addition to its physical benefits, tennis has also been found to encourage sound psychological well-being through its social aspect. As players interact with each other on the court they develop relationships that can last throughout life; bonds that are based on shared passions and common interests rather than superficial conversations.

◆ Amateur tennis players enjoy the thrill of competing against an opponent who shares similar goals— whether it's playing for fun or striving for victory— and being part of a larger community of like-minded individuals who share the same values when it comes to enjoying the game of tennis. There is something special about going out onto a court surrounded by nature—fresh air filled with birds singing—where participants come together in pursuit of achieving a common goal: having fun!

This statue of Fred Perry located at the Tennis Hall of Fame is a replicate of the one that stands inside the Church Road gate at the All England Lawn Tennis Club in Wimbledon. Erected in 1984, it marked the 50th anniversary of his first singles championship.

Women in Tennis

Women have been playing tennis since the late 19th century, but it wasn't until the 20th century that they began to make a name for themselves in the sport. In the early 1900s, female tennis players were limited to country club tournaments and were not allowed to compete in major international events such as Wimbledon or the U.S. Open. Even when women did manage to find their way onto a major tournament court, they were often subjected to unfair treatment and ridicule from male players and spectators alike.

Near the beginning of the 20th century, female tennis players began making strides towards equality on and off the court. One of these pioneers in women's tennis was American world champion Molla Mallory, who won 8 US National singles titles between 1915 and 1926, helping to raise public interest in women's tennis along the way. She also helped found the Women's National Tennis Association (WNTA) in 1923, which gave female players more recognition and opportunities than ever before.

The 1950s saw a massive surge of interest in women's tennis as world-renowned female athletes like Maureen Connolly Brinker, Althea Gibson and Doris Hart made history with their success on the court. In 1957, Connolly became the first woman ever to win all four Grand Slam titles in a single season; she went on to become one of only four women in history who have achieved this feat (along with Serena Williams, Margaret Court and Steffi Graf). Gibson followed suit by becoming the first African American player—man or woman—to win a Grand Slam title at Wimbledon in 1957; her accomplishments helped open doors for future black athletes across all sports.

In 1968, Billie Jean King changed everything when she founded The Women's Tennis Association (WTA), an organization that continues to serve as an advocate for female athletes today. She was integral in advocating for equal prize money for men and women at major tournaments throughout her career; it finally happened at Wimbledon in 2007 after decades of fighting for equal rights on and off court. This victory was huge for female players everywhere as it meant they could finally receive just compensation for their hard work regardless of gender—something that had previously been unheard of up until then.

Today, professional women's tennis has seen some incredible highs with record-breaking names like Serena Williams leading some of greatest eras in professional sports; but there is still work to be done when it comes to equality on tour. While pay discrepancies between men and women are slowly narrowing due primarily to increased sponsorship deals targeting female players specifically (something which King herself campaigned tirelessly for during her career), there is still much progress to be made regarding sexism within professional tennis circles— particularly for those competing on lower tiers than Grand Slam events where prize money remains significantly lower than its male counterpart counterparts despite greater efforts from organizations like WTA Tour & ITF Futures Series Tours at bridging that gap with improved rules and regulations . Hopefully one day soon we will see true parity between men's and women's pro-

Throughout the history of tennis, there have been many incredible female players who have left their mark on the sport. The women who dominate the game are highly talented athletes with a relentless drive to succeed

fessional tennis—both on court and off—allowing us all witness some truly legendary matches and moments from our favorite athletes!

Throughout the history of tennis, there have been many incredible female players who have left their mark on the sport. The women who dominate the game are highly talented athletes with a relentless drive to succeed and an unyielding passion for the game. From Martina Navratilova and Billie Jean King to Steffi Graf and Serena and Venus Williams.

Among the greatest female tennis players in history, Martina Navratilova and Billie Jean King are often recognized as pioneers of the sport. Known for her hard-hitting style of play, Navratilova won a staggering 167 singles titles during her career and was particularly dominant from 1983 to 1987. She became the first woman ever to win more than $20 million in prize money and held the top spot in women's tennis for an impressive 332 weeks. Billie Jean King is another iconic figure who revolutionized women's tennis with her on-court accomplishments, including 12 Grand Slam singles titles, 16 Grand Slam doubles titles, and 11 Grand Slam mixed doubles championships.

Steffi Graf is another name that stands out among the greatest female tennis champions of all time. During her illustrious career, she racked up 107 singles titles, 22 doubles titles, and 7 gold medals in major tournaments. Her 1988 "Golden Slam"—when she swept all four Grand Slam events plus Olympic gold—remains one of the most impressive achievements in sports history.

One cannot talk about female tennis titans without mentioning Serena Williams — one of the greatest athletes ever to grace a court. She has gone down in history as one of the most successful women's players of all time. Her power and athleticism have been remarkable to watch over the years.

Additionally, there are other greats such as Monica Seles, Justine Henin, Chris Evert, Lindsay Davenport and Martina Hingis who have made huge contributions to women's tennis over the years. By consistently pushing each other through their high caliber performances both on and off the court, these champions have set an inspiring example for generations of aspiring players to come.

Women's Best Players

and Millions More

MELBOURNE, AUSTRALIA—JANUARY 26, 2016: Twenty one times Grand Slam champion Serena Williams in action during her quarter final match at Australian Open 2016 at Australian tennis center in Melbourne

SERENA WILLIAMS

Serena Williams was born in Michigan. She began playing tennis at the age of 3. Her father relocated the family to Compton, California and was home—schooled. According to her father's autobiography, he reasoned that the difficult environment in Compton would "make them tough, give them a fighter's mentality."

"I really think a champion is defined not by their wins but how they can recover when they fall." SERENA WILLIAMS

Serena Williams is widely regarded as one of the greatest tennis players of all time. She has been ranked world number one in singles by the Women's Tennis Association on eight occasions between 2002 and 2017. She has won a total of 72 WTA singles titles, including 23 Grand Slam singles titles—more than any other player in history. During her career, she has reached thirty-one major finals, the most for any tennis player in the Open Era.

In addition to her Grand Slam titles, Williams is also a five-time champion at the WTA Tour Championships, four-time Olympic gold medalist, and 14-time winner of year-end WTA Tour Finals. She was also the first African American woman to win a Grand Slam title in singles when she won the 1999 US Open. In 2015, she became only the fourth female player to hold all four major titles simultaneously after Steffi Graf, Martina Navratilova and Maureen Connolly Brinker.

Her rivalry with Maria Sharapova is considered to be one of the most iconic rivalries in sports history and she holds numerous records for having played more Grand Slam tournament matches than any other female player in history.

Do You Know?

Serena Williams

◆ In 2020, Serena became the first Black woman to become a co-owner of a professional sports team when she acquired a stake in NFL team Miami Dolphins.

◆ Throughout her career, Serena has always been a vocal advocate for women's rights and racial justice. She created The Yetunde Price Resource Center (named after her late sister) to help families affected by violence in Compton, California; launched an initiative called 'Aneres' which provides resources for underprivileged girls; and raised money for various charities with her "Serena Slam" tour—where she played tennis against celebrity opponents with all proceeds going towards charity.

◆ She is the only player, male or female, to accomplish a Career Golden Slam in both singles and doubles.

◆ She became just the second African-American woman to triumph in a singles Grand Slam match. Williams, 17 years old, defeated Swiss Miss Martina Hingis in the 1999 US Open championship match, 6-3, 7-6. (4). Williams won the tournament's final five matches by defeating several players, including Kim Clijsters, Lindsay Davenport, and Martina Hingis.

◆ In 2009, Williams released her autobiography Titled, My Life: Queen of the Court. The book tells us about her personal life and career in tennis. Williams also co-authored a book titled Venus and Serena: Serving from the Hip with her sister.

BILLIE JEAN KING

Billie Jean King is one of the most renowned figures in the history of tennis. She is known for her pioneering contributions to gender equality in sports, as well as her tremendous success on the court. King began playing tennis at a young age and later won 39 Grand Slam titles during her career, becoming one of the most decorated players in the sport. In 1973, she famously defeated Bobby Riggs in the Battle of the Sexes match, an event watched by over 50 million people around the world.

Throughout her life, King has been an outspoken advocate for equality, both on and off the court. In 1972 she founded the Women's Tennis Association (WTA) and served as its first president. She also created World Team Tennis (WTT), a professional league that combines men and women equally on teams, even before Title IX was passed into law. Billie Jean has been celebrated with numerous awards throughout her career from organizations such as ESPN, Sports Illustrated, and People magazine for accomplishments like being named 'The Greatest Female Tennis Player of All Time' by Tennis magazine in 2009.

In addition to her many victories on court and advocacy off it, King was inducted into both The International Tennis Hall of Fame and World Golf Hall of Fame in 1987 and 2000 respectively—the only athlete to be awarded this honor twice! To this day, she remains an inspirational figure in tennis due to her spirit of determination and commitment to inspiring change through sports.

DO YOU KNOW?

Billie Jean King

◆ Billie Jean King was the first female tennis player to earn over $100,000 in prize money. She also became the first female athlete to receive a million-dollar endorsement contract when she signed with Bristol-Myers in 1972.

◆ She was awarded an honorary knighthood from Queen Elizabeth II in 1990 for her dedication and commitment towards promoting gender equality both within sport and society.

◆ Billie Jean King was the first female player to win the 'Wimbledon' singles title in 1968.

◆ She won the "Battles of the Sexes" match against Don Riggs 6–4, 6–3, 6–3. This match brought women's tennis into mainstream media attention and helped propel gender equality forward.

◆ Thirty thousand tennis fans witnessed the Battle of the Sexes match at the Astrodome in Houston, Texas and 90 million watched the match on television.

◆ She attended LA State College for three years and there she met future husband Larry King, whom she married in 1965. It was here that Billie Jean's eyes began to open up to the inequalities faced by women in society. As a talented amateur player, she was denied access to a college scholarship simply because she was female. Her first success came in 1961 while still at college; she won the Wimbledon doubles championship with partner Karen Hantze on their first attempt, becoming the youngest team to win.

MARTINA NAVRATILOVA

Martina Navratilova born on October 18, 1956, is a Czech–American former professional tennis player. Widely considered among the greatest tennis players of all time, Navratilova won 18 major singles titles, 31 major women's doubles titles, and 10 major mixed doubles titles, for a combined total of 59 major titles, the most in the Open Era. Alongside Chris Evert, her greatest rival, Navratilova dominated women's tennis in the 1970s and 1980s.

Navratilova was ranked as the world No. 1 in singles for a total of 332 weeks (second only to Steffi Graf), and for a record 237 weeks in doubles, making her the only player in history to have held the top spot in both disciplines for over 200 weeks. She won 167 top-level singles titles and 177 doubles titles; both the Open Era records. She won a record six consecutive singles majors across 1983 and 1984 while simultaneously winning the Grand Slam in doubles. Navratilova claims the best professional season winning percentage, 98.8% in 1983 (going 98–1 for the season), and the longest all-surface winning streak of 74 straight match wins. She reached the Wimbledon singles final 12 times, including for nine consecutive years from 1982 through 1990, and won the title a record nine times. Navratilova is one of the three tennis players, along with Margaret Court and Doris Hart, to have accomplished a career Grand Slam in singles, same-sex doubles, and mixed doubles, called the career "Boxed Set". She won her last major title, the mixed doubles crown at the 2006 US Open, shortly before her 50th birthday, and 32 years after her first major title in 1974.

Originally from Czechoslovakia, Navratilova was stripped of her citizenship when, in 1975 at age 18, she asked the United States for political asylum and was granted temporary residence. She became a US citizen in 1981. On January 9, 2008, Navratilova acquired Czech citizenship, thus becoming a dual citizen. She stated she has not renounced her U.S. citizenship, nor does she plan to do so, and that reclaiming Czech nationality was not politically motivated. Navratilova has been openly lesbian since 1981 and has been an activist for LGBT issues.

DO YOU KNOW?

Martina Navratilova

- She was so focused that she often practiced for up to nine hours a day in preparation for major tournaments. In addition, she was one of very few players to switch from forehand to two-handed backhand mid-match if it meant increasing her chances of winning.

- Aside from her impressive achievements on the court, Navratilova has been an outspoken advocate for human rights issues such as gay rights and HIV awareness since coming out as a lesbian early in her career.

- Martina also wrote, with Liz Nickles, a series of mysteries centered on the character Jordan Myles, a former tennis champion turned sleuth. The Total Zone (1994) was followed by Breaking Point (1996) and Killer Instinct (1997).

STEFFI GRAF

Steffi Graf is one of the most success-ful female tennis players in history. She won 22 Grand Slam singles titles, behind only Serena Williams and Marga-ret Court. She was the first female player to achieve a 'Golden Slam'—winning all four Grand Slams plus an Olympic gold medals in 1988.

Graf was renowned for her outstanding style of play, which combined speed, power, and finesse with impressive court coverage. She won six French Open titles, seven Wimbledon titles, five US Open titles, and four Australian Open titles throughout her career. Her 1992 victory at the French Open made her the only player ever to win each Grand Slam event at least four times.

> *"You can't measure success if you have never failed. My father has taught me that if you really do want to reach your goals, you can't spend any time worrying about whether you're going to win or lose. Focus only on getting better."—STEFFI GRAF*

Graf was also one of the great doubles players of her era and won six women's doubles major championships with partner Pam Shriver. In addition to being a multiple Grand Slam champion in singles and doubles, Graf was also a two-time WTA Tour Championships winner and won 17 Tier I singles events as well as three team championships with Germany in Fed Cup competition. She retired from professional tennis in 1999 after winning 107 career singles titles and eleven doubles titles during her illustrious career.

Do You Know?

Steffi Graff

◆ Since 2006 Steffi Graff and her foundation, Children for Tomorrow, has provided psychological support to children who are victims of war and violence around the world.

◆ Steffi Graf was also inducted into the International Tennis Hall of Fame in 2004 at age 34—making her one of youngest people ever to receive this honor.

◆ She was coached by her father Peter Graf, who had a great influence on her career. Under his tutelage, she won her first professional tournament at the age of thirteen.

◆ She held the world number one ranking for a record weeks during her career.

◆ Steffi Graf retired from professional tennis in 1999 at the age of 30. After retiring, she remained active in the sport, coaching and mentoring young players. She also established the Steffi Graf Youth Tennis Center in Leipzig, Germany, which provides training and resources for young tennis players.

◆ In addition to her involvement in tennis, Graf has also been involved in various philanthropic and humanitarian efforts. She is the founder of Children for Tomorrow, a non-profit organization dedicated to supporting children who have experienced trauma and violence. Graf has also been involved in fundraising efforts for disaster relief and environmental causes.

MARGARET COURT

Margaret Court is one of the most successful tennis players of all time and holds a total of 64 Grand Slam titles across singles, doubles, and mixed doubles. She was the first player to win the 'Grand Slam' by winning all four major championships in a single year (1970). During her career she won a total of 24 Grand Slam singles titles—more than any other female tennis player in history—and 11 Grand Slam doubles titles.

Court also won two Australian Open singles titles, 10 French Open women's singles titles, five Wimbledon women's singles titles and seven US Open women's singles titles. She also holds

the record for having achieved the longest winning streak in professional tennis history with 74 consecutive match wins. In addition to her success on court, Court also experienced great success off court as well. She has worked as an author and coach since retiring from professional tennis in 1977.

Court was inducted into the International Tennis Hall of Fame in 1979 and she is widely regarded as one of the greatest players ever to have played the sport. Her rivalry with Billie Jean King is considered to be one of the most iconic rivalries in sports history and she continues to hold numerous records for having played more matches than any other female player in history.

Do You Know?

Margaret Court

◆ In 1970, she became the first woman athlete to win the prestigious Sports Illustrated "Sportswoman of the Year" award.

◆ She was appointed as an Officer of The Order of Australia in 2007 for her services to tennis and dedication towards promoting gender equality both within sport and society as a whole.

◆ She holds the record for most titles, ranked number one for more than 200 weeks and played in over 700 tournaments.

◆ She is also an ordained minister and evangelical Christian. She founded private Christian schools— the Margaret Court Bible College in Perth and the Victory Life Centre Church in Armadale—and published books on religion and parenting.

◆ In 1970 Margaret Court became the first woman during the Open Era (the second woman in history after Maureen Connolly to win the singles Grand Slam.

◆ Margaret Court retired from professional tennis in 1977 and focused on her family and her church ministry. She became a Christian minister and, along with her husband Barry, founded the Victory Life Centre, a Pentecostal church in Perth, Australia. Court also established a tennis academy to help young players develop their skills.

CHRIS EVERT

Christine Marie Evert was born December 21, 1954), known as Chris Evert Lloyd from 1979 to 1987, is an American former world No. 1 tennis player. Evert won 18 major singles titles, including a record seven French Open titles and a joint-record six US Open titles (tied with Serena Williams). She was ranked world No. 1 for 260 weeks and was the year-end world No. 1 singles player seven times (1974–78, 1980, 1981). Alongside Martina Navratilova, her greatest rival, Evert dominated women's tennis in the 1970s and 1980s.

"If you can react the same way to winning and losing, that's a big accomplishment. That quality is important because it stays with you the rest of your life."—CHRIS EVERT

Evert reached thirty-four major singles finals, the most in history. In singles, Evert reached the semifinals or better in 52 of the 56 majors she played, including at 34 consecutive majors entered from the 1971 US Open through the 1983 French Open. She never lost in the first or second round of a major and lost in the third round only twice. She holds the record of most consecutive years (13) of winning at least one major title. Evert's career winning percentage in singles matches of 89.97% (1309–146) is the second highest in the Open Era, for men or women. On clay courts, her career winning percentage in singles matches of 94.55% (382–22) remains a WTA Tour record. She also won three major doubles titles.

Evert served as president of the WTA for eleven years, 1975–76 and 1983–91. She was awarded the Philippe Chatrier award and inducted into the Hall of Fame. In later life, Evert was a coach and is now an analyst for ESPN.

Do You Know?

Chris Evert

◆ Chris Evert also holds several records for being the youngest player to achieve certain milestones in her career: she was the youngest winner of a non-senior ladies' tournament (age 14), the first female teenager to win a Grand Slam title (at age 18), and the youngest person to be ranked world number 1 (age 19).

◆ Not only did Chris Evert win on the court; off it, she helped found The Chris Evert Charities which supports underprivileged children around Florida by providing them access to recreational activities such as tennis clinics. Since its inception in 1986, The Chris Evert Charities has raised over $20 million for children's charities.

◆ Chris Evert has been inducted into multiple halls of fame including both the International Tennis Hall of Fame and International Women's Sports Hall of Fame. She was named one of ESPN's "50 Greatest Players" in 2009.

◆ She was the first player, male or female, to win 1,000 singles matches Her career match wins total 1,309, second only to Martina Navratilova's record of 1,442.

◆ After retiring from tennis in 1989, Chris Evert continued to be involved in the sport as a commentator and analyst for major tennis tournaments. She also founded the Evert Tennis Academy, which provides tennis training for young players.

VENUS WILLIAMS

Venus Williams has won seven Grand Slam singles titles, five at Wimbledon and two at the US Open. She is widely regarded as one of the all-time greats of the sport.

Along with her younger sister, Serena, Venus Williams was coached by her parents Oracene Price and Richard Williams. Turning professional in 1994, she reached her first major final at the 1997 US Open. In 2000 and 2001, Williams claimed the Wimbledon and US Open titles, as well as Olympic singles gold at the 2000 Sydney Olympics.

She first reached the singles world No. 1 ranking on 25 February 2002, becoming the first African American woman to do so in the Open era, and the second of all-time after Althea Gibson. [8] She reached four consecutive major finals between 2002 and 2003, but lost each time to Serena. She then suffered from injuries, winning just one major title between 2003 and 2006.

"You have to let fear go. Another lesson is you just have to believe in yourself; you just have to. There's no way around it. No matter how things are stacked against you."—VENUS WILLIAMS

Williams returned to form starting in 2007, when she won Wimbledon (a feat she repeated the following year). In 2010, she returned to the world No. 2 position in singles, but then suffered again from injuries. Starting in 2014, she again gradually returned to form, culminating in two major final appearances at the Australian Open and Wimbledon in 2017.

Do You Know?

Venus Williams

- As an amateur, Venus Williams never lost a match on the United States Tennis Association Junior Tour. Her record was 63-0.

- Venus Williams was 14 years old when she competed in her first career professional tennis match in 1994.

- Venus has a fashion degree from the Art Institute of Fort Lauderdale.

- Her combined total of 73 WTA titles is also second among active players behind Serena.

- She has earned forty-two million as a tennis player.

Grand Slam champion Venus Williams of United States during press conference after her first round match at US Open 2016.

THE REST OF THE BEST

All of the players listed below are among the greatest of all time, the women listed above are subjective choices. Here are those that complete the best of all time.

Monica Seles, Evonne Goolagong Cawley, Justine Henin, Martina Hingis, Helen Wills Moody, Maureen Connolly, Lindsay Davenport, Kim Clijsters, Jennifer Capriati, Maria Sharapova, Tracy Austin, Simona Halep, Amelie Mauresmo

Brynn Freeman, 19, and Mother Katherin Nukk-Freeman at the Bath and Tennis Club in Spring Lake New Jersey.

There are some players making a career with their tennis skills and some will emerge as champions supplanting those currently at the top.

And then there is the majority of women who play for a variety of reasons including fun.

Women have been playing tennis since the late 19th century, when women's tennis first became popular in England. Nowadays, tennis is a sport that is enjoyed by both men and women of all ages around the world.

Women who have made their passion for the game last throughout their lives often display great physical conditioning and technical skill due to years of honing their technique and building up strength. Many veteran female players are still able to compete at high levels well into their senior years while still being able to enjoy a fun match with friends or family members.

Majbritt Quigley, Sandy Manley, Joni Stone, Meghan van Vliet, Newburyport, MA.

In addition to its physical benefits, playing tennis throughout life can also provide mental stimulation and social connections. Long-term players are exposed to different strategies and tactics as they progress through different stages of ability, which helps them develop problem-solving skills and an appreciation for the nuances of the game. The camaraderie amongst long-term players can also provide an important sense of community with those who share mutual interests, especially when faced with changing climates like aging or relocation.

As more women recognize both the physical and mental health benefits associated with consistent participation in sports such as tennis, more are committing themselves to taking part in this timeless activity on a regular basis. Whether it's joining a local league team or just scheduling time for recreational play every week, taking up or continuing a lifelong relationship with tennis can definitely add value and enjoyment to one's life journey.

*Front cover of **Le Miroir des sports**, first issue July 8th, 1920, with Suzanne Lenglen and Gerald Patterson.*

Women in the Tennis Hall of Fame
Who Made a Significant Contribution

Suzanne Lenglen: Class of 1977

The first woman in modern tennis to achieve significant recognition was Suzanne Lenglen. She was born in 1899 in France, and quickly gained fame for her skillful and powerful playing style which soon made her the most successful female tennis player of all time. She won 31 Major singles titles during her career, including six French Open Championships and six Wimbledon Championships

This drive carried over into other areas of her life; during WWI she helped French soldiers while serving as a nurse's aide.

Lenglen's accomplishments were recognized by both fans and peers alike; she won multiple awards such as being voted world champion in 1921 by AELTC (The All England Lawn Tennis & Croquet Club). She was inducted into the International Tennis Hall of Fame in 1977, becoming one of its first female members, and is still considered one of the greatest players in tennis history today.

GLADYS HELDMAN—CLASS OF 1979

Gladys Heldman was the International Tennis Hall of Fame's first female Contributor, and for good reason. She created the Virginia Slims Circuit, the precursor to the WTA. In 1953, as the mother of two young girls, Heldman founded World Tennis magazine.

Along the way, she advocated for equality and as the disparity in prize money offered to the genders grew, the leading women players turned to her for leadership. Heldman responded by rallying her business contacts to stage the Virginia Slims Invitational in Houston in September 1970, signing nine players to emblematic $1 contracts.

MARY OUTERBRIDGE—CLASS OF 1981

Time shrouds the details in mystery, but Mary Ewing Outerbridge is widely considered to be the "Mother of American Tennis." As a young woman, Outerbridge encountered the sport while on vacation in Bermuda in 1874—the story goes that she saw British army officers playing the newly patented game of lawn tennis and they gave her a set of equipment to take home to New York. Outerbridge set up an hourglass-shaped court at the Staten Island Cricket and Baseball Club and played what may well have been the first tennis match in America against her sister, Laura. game. Mary didn't live to see how the sport would grow. She died in 1886 at the age of 34.

PEACHY KELLMEYER—CLASS OF 2011

Peachy Kellmeyer goes down in history as the first employee of the Women's Tennis Association (WTA). She was hired as the new body's Tour Director in 1973. In the years that followed,

Kellmeyer played a principal executive role, generating business growth and a regulatory structure for the tour, while never letting up in the battle for equal prize money. Before all that, the West Virginia native enjoyed a successful junior career and was the first woman to play on the men's Division I tennis team at the University of Miami.

JANE BROWN GRIMES—CLASS OF 2014

Hired in the 1970s to develop the scope and prestige of the International Tennis Hall of Fame—which meant everything from building the museum's collection to overseeing the restoration of historic buildings at Newport—Jane Brown Grimes went on to hold myriad leadership and committee roles across the WTA, United States Tennis Association (USTA) and International Tennis Federation (ITF).

NANCY JEFFETT—CLASS OF 2015

One of the first promoters of women's professional tennis and a longtime chair of the U.S. Wightman Cup and Fed Cup competitions, Nancy Jeffett is also celebrated for her lifetime commitment to juniors and player development. She built a reputation for getting things done on the Texas tennis scene and Jeffett befriended Maureen "Little Mo" Connolly when the Grand Slam-winning great. In 1968, the duo co-founded the Maureen Connolly Brinker Tennis Foundation, and although Connolly died from cancer soon after, Jeffett spent the next four decades fostering young talent through individual and team competitions for girls and boys, right up to the international level.

*"What we did in 1970, we did on our own —
and with little or no support from the tennis
establishment. They wanted to throw us
out, but we have persevered — and today,
every time the names Williams, Sharapova,
Halep or any of today's great champions are
etched into the history of women's tennis, I
hope history will recognize that they are not
only worthy, but they are standing on the
shoulders of history."*—BILLY JEAN KING

The Original 9

Nine Women Professional Tennis Players Who Broke Away from the Governing Bodies of Tennis

THE ORIGINAL 9 —Rosie Casals ,Billie Jean King, Valerie Ziegenfuss, Kristy Pigeon,Nancy Richey ,Julie Heldman ,Peaches Bartkowicz,Kerry Reid and Judy Dalton.

THE ORIGINAL 9

The Original 9 were a group of nine women's professional tennis players who broke away from the governing bodies of tennis in 1970, by signing $1.00 contracts with Gladys Heldman, to launch their own tour. Men had rejected their request for better pay. The nine women included Billie Jean King, Rosie Casals, Julie Heldman, Valerie Ziegenfuss, Judy Tegart Dalton, Kerry Melville Reid, Peaches Bartkowicz, Kristy Pigeon, and Nancy Richey. They are famous for being the pioneers of women's professional tennis and for standing up for equal pay and treatment in the sport.

At the time, female athletes were not given the same opportunities or recognition as male athletes. The Original 9 decided to take a stand and formed their own tour which was eventually taken over by the Women's Tennis Association (WTA). This allowed them to have more control over their careers and gave them an opportunity to make a living playing tennis.

The Original 9 also fought for equal prize money between men and women in tennis tournaments. In 1973 they won their fight when the US Open became the first Grand Slam tournament to offer equal prize money. This was a major victory that paved the way for other female athletes to be treated with respect and receive fair compensation for their work.

The Original 9 are remembered as trailblazers who changed the landscape of professional sports forever. Their courage and determination set an example that has inspired generations of female athletes since then.

DO YOU KNOW?

The Original 9

◆ **Rosie Casals** was the first winner of a Virginia Slims tournament played in Houston Texas. The profit for the tournament was $850.00.

◆ **Billie Jean King** in 1974 founded the Women's Sports Foundation and became the first female player-coach of a professional team when she led the Freedoms for the initial season of World Team Tennis.

◆ **Valerie Ziegenfuss** was among the first tennis professionals to us the Prince oversize racket.

◆ **Kristy Pigeon** retired from tennis after two years and retired to Sun Valley Idaho where she ran a tennis school.

◆ **Nancy Richey** was inducted int the International Tennis Hall of Fame in 2003.

◆ **Julie Heldman** entered UCLA Law School after she retired in 1978. She was elected editor of the Law Review.

◆ **Peaches Bartkowicz** received financial assistance from the WTA for a caretaker to help her recover from bone marrow transplant.

◆ **Kerry Reid** won the women's singles title at the Australian Open in 1977.

◆ **Judy Dalton** became President of the Australian Fed Cup Foundation that helps provide tennis opportunities for girls in Australia.

- The Original 9 signed their one dollar contracts a year before Title IX was passed.

- As a result of their groundbreaking efforts, the Original 9 were banned from playing in major tournaments for a time, but their persistence eventually paid off when the Grand Slam tournaments began offering equal prize money to men and women.

- The Original 9 agreed to participate in the Virginia Slims series with the first tournament to be held in Houston.

"We, as the Original Nine, were not doing it for ourselves," said King. "Without it, I would not have been who I am. Never in 100 years would I have had the life I have without the nine of us all sticking together. — BILLY JEAN KING

The Grand Slam
Tournaments

Tennis Grand Slam tournaments, or major championships as they are sometimes referred to, have been around since the 19th century. The first of these was in 1877 when the Wimbledon tournament began in England. Initially a men's singles and doubles event, it soon grew to include women's competitions and mixed doubles play as well. This was soon followed by the US Open in 1881 with the French Open starting in 1925 and finally the Australian Open beginning in 1905.

""I was a little bit lost in my head after winning a Grand Slam. You're like: 'So what's the next goal? What do you want now? Where do you want to be? It's not a problem if you lose."—STAN WAWRINKA

Over the years tennis Grand Slam tournaments have seen many changes in both their format and rules. In 1968, for example, all four Majors adopted an open era allowing professional players to compete against amateurs for titles. The same year saw the introduction of a tiebreaker scoring system which had previously been used only at Wimbledon and allowed matches to be completed more quickly without having to resort to playing games out until one player achieved a two-game lead. Players during this time adapted their style of play quickly to make use of this new system, leading direct points rather than relying on long rallies as before.

In recent years, the three remaining Grand Slam events following Australia's withdrawal from amateur competition have seen further changes such as their move into digital broadcast systems, allowing fans all over the world access to watch matches live or on demand via subscription services. With prize money also increasing throughout these tournaments, many of today's top players now see them as a key part of their earning potential rather than just competing for glory alone.

The Grand Slam tournaments are regulated by the International Tennis Federation (ITF).

The term 'Grand Slam' originates from the card game contract bridge, where it is used for winning all possible tricks, and entered tennis via golf, where it was used for the first time to specifically describe a total of 4 wins, specifically Bobby Jones' achievement of winning the four major golf tournaments three years earlier in 1930. "Grand Slam" or "Slam" has since also become used to refer to the tournaments individually.

The history of professional tennis Grand Slam tournaments is long and varied but one thing remains true: these four major championships continue to be some of the most prestigious events in all of sports today with millions tuning in every year from all corners of globe to witness history being made.

Do You Know?

The Grand Slam

- In 2018, the tournament was the first Grand Slam tournament that introduced the shot clock to keep a check on the time consumed by players between points. The reason for this change was to increase the pace of play. The clock is placed in a position visible to players, the chair umpire, and fans. From 2020, all Grand Slams, ATP, and WTA tournaments apply this technology.

- Tiebreakers standardized for all, when a match reaches 6–all in the last possible set (the third for women and fifth for men), an extended tiebreaker (first to 10 points, win by 2) is played. Hence, should the tiebreaker be even at 9-all, whoever scores two straight points wins the match and/or championship.

- Tensions over this status quo, which had been building for decades, finally came to a head in 1967. In an experiment, the first tournament open to professional tennis players played on Centre Court at Wimbledon, the Wimbledon Pro, was staged by the All England Lawn Tennis Club in August, offering a prize fund of $45,000 US. The tournament was deemed very successful, with packed crowds and the play seen as being of higher quality than the amateur-only Wimbledon final held two weeks earlier.

- In 1968 players of all statuses were admitted to the 1968 Wimbledon Championships and other future tournaments.

◆ It was the start of the Open Era of tennis.

◆ Although it has been possible to complete a Grand Slam in most years and most disciplines since 1925, it was not possible from 1940 to 1945 because of interruptions at Wimbledon, the Australian and French Championships due to World War II, the years from 1970 to 1985 when there was no Australian tournament in mixed doubles, 1986 when there was no Australian Open, and 2020 when Wimbledon was cancelled due to the COVID-19 pandemic.

Maria Sharapova— Five-time Grand Slam champion.

◆ Don Budge's first ever "Grand Slam" in 1938 to Roger Federer's six consecutive titles from 2004-2008—but no player has had as lasting an impact as Billie Jean King: namesake for the National Tennis Center and winner of 12 grand slam singles titles throughout her career (six at Wimbledon and four at the US Open).

◆ In 1976 she upset Bobby Riggs in what became known as "the Battle of the Sexes" setting a powerful example for female athletes everywhere that continues to inspire today.

The Australian Open

The Australian Open is a tennis tournament held annually at Melbourne Park in Melbourne, Victoria, Australia. The tournament is the first of the four Grand Slam tennis events held each year, preceding the French Open, Wimbledon, and the US Open. The Australian Open starts in the middle of January and continues for two weeks coinciding with the Australia Day holiday. It features men's and women's singles; men's, women's, and mixed doubles; junior's championships; and wheelchair, legends, and exhibition events. Before 1988, it was played on grass courts.

The Australian Open is managed by Tennis Australia, formerly the Lawn Tennis Association of Australia (LTAA), and was first played at the Warehouseman's Cricket Ground in Melbourne in November 1905. The facility is now known as the Albert Reserve Tennis Centre.

The tournament was first known as the Australasian Championships. It became the Australian Championships in 1927. Then, in 1969, it became the Australian Open. Since 1905, it has been staged 110 times in five Australian cities: Melbourne (66 times), Sydney (17 times), Adelaide (15 times), Brisbane (7 times), Perth

(3 times), and two New Zealander cities: Christchurch (1906) and Hastings (1912).

During World War II, the tournament was not held in the period from 1941 to 1945. In 1972, it was decided to stage the tournament in Melbourne each year because it attracted the biggest patronage of any Australian city. The tournament was played at the Kooyong Lawn Tennis Club from 1972 until its move to the new Flinders Park complex in 1988.

The Facility

The new facilities at Flinders Park were envisaged to meet the demands of a tournament that had outgrown Kooyong's capacity. The move to Flinders Park was an immediate success, with a 90 percent increase in attendance in 1988 (266,436) on the previous year at Kooyong (140,000).

In 2008 Melbourne Park precinct commenced upgrades which enhanced facilities for players and spectators.

The main arena is the Rod Laver Arena, and it has a capacity of approximately 15,000 spectators. It has a retractable roof.

Notably a retractable roof was placed over Margaret Court Arena, making the Open the first of the four Grand Slams to have retractable roofs available on three of their main courts. The player and administrative facilities, as well as access points for spectators, were improved and the tournament site expanded its footprint out of Melbourne Park into nearby Birrarung Marr. A fourth major show court, seating 5,000 people was completed in late 2021, along with the rest of decade-long redevelopment, which included the Centrepiece ballroom, function and media building, as well as other upgraded facilities for players, administrators and spectators.

In 2021, in an effort to reduce the number of staff on-site due to the COVID-19 pandemic, all matches used electronic line judging. It marked the first-ever Grand Slam tournament to exclusively use electronic line judging.

The project also built a real-life replica of the precinct in Decentraland where people could spectate and interact with each other in real time. The Australian Open Artball NFTs generated over $5 million in revenue and won a Cannes Lions Award for Sports Entertainment.

The Court Surface

Since 2008, all of the courts used during the Australian Open are hard courts with Plexicushion acrylic surfaces (though Melbourne Park does have eight practice clay courts these are not used for the tournament). This replaced the Rebound Ace surface used from the opening of Melbourne Park. The ITF rated the surface's speed as medium.

The Trophies

Norman Brooks Challenge Cup (Men's) is named after the late Sir Norman Brookes (1877-1968), a former Australian tennis champion. It was first awarded to Fred Perry at the Australian Championships in 1934.

The Sir Norman Brookes Challenger Cup is based on a large Roman marble vase, excavated from the ruins of Emperor Hadrian's villa outside Rome. Since the vase found a resting place in Warwick Castle, it is known as the Warwick vase. The winner gets a 3/4th size replica of it. The diameter of the bowl is 25.7cm and the width including the handles is 39cm. The height of the trophy is 28cm and stands on a plinth of 15.5cm.

Daphne Akhurst Memorial Cup (Women's) is named after the late Daphne Akhurst (1903—1933), a five times singles cham-

Australian Open—There are two perpetual trophies presented to each of the male and female singles winners of the Australian Open.

pion and was first awarded to Joan Hartigan at the Australian Championships in 1934.

Trophies are on display for public viewing near the new AO Game hub in Garden Square during the tournament in the afternoon.

The winners receive a replica of the Daphne Akhurst Memorial Cup. Silver gilt was used to make the trophy which is eighteen inches tall and 7.5 cm in diameter. The Australian Open winners get to see their names imprinted on the trophy after the final alongside former champions.

Do You Know?

The Australian Open

◆ Even in the 1960s and 1970s, when travel was less difficult, leading players such as Manuel Santana, Jan Kodeš, Manuel Orantes, avoided the tournament. Ilie Năstase (who only came once, when 35 years old) and Björn Borg came rarely or not at all.

◆ Mats Wilander was the only player to win the tournament on both grass and hard courts.

◆ Martina Hingis won the women's singles title in 1997, aged 16 years and three months. She would go on to reach the final of every major tournament that year, winning all but the French Open.

◆ Three women have won the singles titles three times. They are Steffi Graf, Martina Hingis, and Monica Seles.

◆ Serena Williams won the women's singles title seven times.

◆ The Australian Open has an Extreme Heat Policy. Introduced in 1998, it calls for play to be stopped on all courts once the temperature reaches 104 degrees F (40 degrees C). In 2014, the temperatures during the Open ranged from 106.7-111.02 degrees F (41.5-43.9 degrees C). Although the organizers claimed that the humidity was low and that the play could continue, nine players withdrew from the first round.

◆ Roger Federer and Serena Williams are the only players to win the Australian Open on both Rebound Ace and Plexicushion Prestige.

- Each year, the tournament uses around 40,000 tennis balls. To handle them, 360 ball boys and girls selected after an application every year. They are not paid but receive a gift pack and food allowance.

- The first tennis players who came by boats were the US Davis Cup players in November 1946.

- In 2012, the final between Rafael Nadal and Novak Djokovic lasted for 5 hours and 53 minutes, becoming the longest final in Grand Slam history. Novak Djokovic came out as the winner, by 5–7, 6–4, 6–2, 6–7(5–7), 7–5.

- In its early days, the tournament was known as the Australasian Open and the matches were held in five Australian and two New Zealand cities. This makes it the only Grand Slam which has been played in two different countries. In 1972, Melbourne was selected as its official venue and the major has been held here ever since.

- Used tennis balls are sold on the site of the Australian Open and those not sold are given to various groups.

- Dunlop supplies all the tennis balls for use during the Australian Open. Six new balls are used for the five-minute warm-up and the first seven games, with six new balls provided every nine games thereafter.

- The Australian Open started in 1905 and is the youngest of the grand slams.

- When the Australian Open was first held, the very first game was held on a cricket field at the Warehouseman's Cricket Ground. Today, the facility is known as the Albert Reserve Tennis Centre.

DO YOU KNOW
The Australian Open

- The Australian Open is also the first major sporting event to use NFTs (non-fungible token) and the metaverse. The court was split into 6,776 squares that each corresponded to a tennis ball NFt These tennis ball NFTs would change based on where points were scored during the tournament, as determined by the electronic line judging.

- Ken Rosewall is also the youngest p'ayer to win the Australian Open at 18 years old in 1953 and the oldest at 35 in 1972.

- Out of the four Grand Slams, Melbourne Park (Australian Open Venue) is the only venue to have three stadium courts covered by a retractable roof.

- The Australian Open holds the record for the latest ever match conclusion with the Lleyton Hewitt vs Marcos Baghdatis match in 2008 concluding at 4:33am.

- When the tournament was held in Perth, no one from Victoria or New South Wales crossed by train, a distance of about 3,000 kilometres (1,900 mi) between the East and West coasts.

- During a match in 2014, a flock of seagulls flew onto the court and interrupted play for several minutes. The bird refused to leave until officials brought out food to lure it away.

- The Australian Open holds the record for the highest attendance of any tennis tournament ever staged with 812,174 people attending the 2020 edition.

- The Australian Open has been staged twice in New Zealand in 1906 and 1912.

◆ Novak Djokovic has won an all-time record of ten Australian Open men's singles titles. Djokovic is the only male player to win 3 consecutive Australian Open titles during the Open Era, which he has done twice (2011–13 and 2019–21). Margaret Court holds the record for the most Women's Singles Titles with 11 wins.

◆ The Australian Open was the last of the four majors opened to professionals in 1969.

◆ Out of the four Grand Slams, Melbourne Park (Australian Open Venue) is the only venue to have three stadium courts covered by a retractable roof.

◆ The Australian Open holds the record for the latest ever match conclusion with the Lleyton Hewitt vs Marcos Baghdatis match in 2008 concluding at 4:33am.

◆ After winning both his Australian Open Singles titles Jim Courier jumped into the Yarra River for a swim.

◆ The Australian Open was a Grass Court Event until 1988.

◆ Every year the ball kids who work at the Australian Open has a small contingent of overseas ball kids— 20 from Korea, 6 from China, 10 from India and 2 from France.

◆ Over 100 Press Conferences take place over the two weeks of the Australian Open.

◆ The Australian Open is shown live in more than 220 Countries and Territories around the world.

◆ The Australian Open stringers restring over 5000 racquets throughout the tournament using more than 60km's of string.

◆ The highest single-day attendance at the Australian Open is 93,709 at the 2020 edition.

◆ Over 700 Journalists and Photographers cover the Australian Open.

◆ Kia is the longest-running sponsor of the Australian Open beginning it's deal in 2002 with the current deal set to expire in 2023.

◆ The last Australian female to win the Women's Singles Title at the Australian Open was Christine O'Neil in 1978.

◆ The last Australian male to win the Men's Singles Title at the Australian Open was Mark Edmonson in 1976.

◆ From 1905—1968 the tournament was called The Australasian Championships and it became known as the Australian Open in 1969.

◆ Novak Djokovic has won nine Australian Open titles, the most of any male player in the history of the tournament. He could become only the third player in history to secure 10+ titles in a single Grand Slam tournament, after Margaret Court at the Australian Open (11) and Rafael Nadal at the Roland Garros (13).

◆ Artisans created 17 unique, hand-crafted trophies for the winners of each event in 2019, each featuring native Australian flora and fauna.

The French Open is the premier clay court championship in the world and the only Grand Slam tournament currently held on this surface.

The French Open

The French Open (French: Internationaux de France de tennis), also known as Roland-Garros, is a major tennis tournament held over two weeks at the Stade Roland Garros in Paris, France, beginning in late May each year. The tournament and venue are named after the French aviator Roland Garros. The French Open is the premier clay court championship in the world and the only Grand Slam tournament currently held on this surface. It is chronologically the second of the four annual Grand Slam tournaments, occurring after the Australian Open and before Wimbledon and the US Open. Until 1975, the French Open was the only major tournament not played on grass. Between the seven rounds needed for a championship, the clay surface characteristics (slower pace, higher bounce), and the best-of-five-set men's singles matches, the French Open is widely regarded as the most physically demanding tennis tournament in the world.

Officially named in French les Internationaux de France de Tennis (the "French Internationals of Tennis" in English) the tournament itself uses the name Roland-Garros in all languages, and it is usually called the French Open in English.

In 1891 the Championnat de France, which is commonly referred to in English as the French Championships, began. This was only open to tennis players who were members of French clubs. The first women's singles tournament, with four entries, was held in 1897. The mixed doubles event was added in 1902 and the women's doubles in 1907. In the period of 1915–1919, no tournament was organized due to World War I. This tournament was played until 1924, using four venues:

After the Mousquetaires or Philadelphia Four (René Lacoste, Jean Borotra, Henri Cochet, and Jacques Brugnon) won the Davis Cup on American soil in 1927, the French decided to defend the cup in 1928 at a new tennis stadium at Porte d'Auteuil. The Stade de France had offered the tennis authorities three hectares of land with the condition that the new stadium must be named after the World War I aviator hero Roland Garros. The new Stade de Roland Garros (whose central court was renamed Court Philippe Chatrier in 1988) hosted that Davis Cup challenge. On May 24, 1928, the French International Championships moved there, and the event has been held there ever since.

During World War II, the Tournoi de France was not held in 1940 and from 1941 through 1945.. In 1946 and 1947, the French Championships were held after Wimbledon, making it the third Grand Slam event of the year. In 1968, the year of the French General Strike, the French Championships became the first Grand Slam tournament to go open, allowing both amateurs and professionals to compete.

Since 2006 the tournament has begun on a Sunday, featuring 12 singles matches played on the three main courts. Additionally, on the eve of the tournament's opening, the traditional Benny Berthet exhibition day takes place, where the profits go to different charity associations. In March 2007, it was announced that the event would provide equal prize money for both men and women in all rounds for the first time. In 2010, it was announced that the tournament was considering a move away from Roland

Garros as part of a continuing rejuvenation. Plans to renovate and expand Roland Garros have put aside any such consideration, and the tournament remains in its longtime home.

The Court Surface

The French Open has been the only major played on clay court. Clay courts slow down the ball and produce a high bounce when compared with grass courts or hard courts. For this reason, clay courts take away some of the advantages of big servers and serve-and-volleyers, which makes it hard for these types of players to dominate on the surface.

The surface consists of. Red brick dust, crushed white limestone, clinker (coal residue), and crushed drain rock.

The Trophies

The trophies have been awarded to the winners since 1953 and are manufactured by Mellerio dits Meller, a famous Parisian jewelry house. They are all made of pure silver with finely etched decorations on their side. Each new singles winner gets his or her name written on the base of the trophy. Winners receive custom-made pure silver replicas of the trophies they have won They are usually presented by the President of the French Tennis Federation (FFT).

The trophy awarded to the winner of the men's singles is called the Coupe des Mousquetaires (The Musketeers' Cup). It is named in honor of the "Four Musketeers". The trophy weighs 14 kg, is 40 cm high and 19 cm wide. The current design was created in 1981 by the Mellerio dit Meller. Each winner gets a smaller-size replica and the original remains property of the FFT at all times.

The trophy awarded to the winner of the women's singles is called the Coupe Suzanne Lenglen (Suzanne Lenglen Cup) since 1979. The current cup was awarded for the first time in 1986. It is, with a few details, a replica of a cup offered at the time by the city of Nice to Suzanne Lenglen. This trophy, donated by Suzanne Lenglen's family to the Musée National du Sport, was awarded between 1979 and 1985 to every winner until the FFT made a copy. Each winner receives a smaller-size replica and the original remains property of the FFT at all times.

Since 1981, new prizes have been presented: the Prix Orange (for the player demonstrating the best sportsmanship and coopera-tive attitude with the press), the Prix Citron (for the player with the strongest character and personality) and the Prix Bourgeon (for the tennis player revelation of the year).

The Facility

The Stade Roland Garros is a 21-acre complex boasting twenty courts. Built in 1928, Court Philippe Chatrier is the centrepiece and seats over 15,000 spectators. The other show court is named after French tennis player Suzanne Lenglen, one of the biggest tennis stars of the 1920s.

Located in the southern part of the Bois de Boulogne in Paris's 16th arrondissement, the Stade Roland-Garros is comprised of 20 courts on 21 acres, the largest of which seats 15,000 spectators. Despite this sprawling size, the tournament feels incredibly intimate. The bleachers are stacked steeply, giving everyone a great view and lending the event a very close-knit vibe. Another distinctive feature of this stadium and tournament are its iconic red clay courts.

Auteull Greenhouses Roland Gaross

DO YOU KNOW?

The French Open

♦ The Centre court has an underground irrigation system, the first of its kind, to control moisture levels within its surface.

♦ Panama hats are popular among men and women in attendance, something that you might want to pick up as a memory of your time in Paris. Players and spectators alike tend to be effortlessly chic and well-dressed at Roland-Garros, so make sure you put some thought into your outfit before you go!

♦ Maintaining the courts requires four full-time employees, and new clay costs more than $2,000 a year for each court. Each court must be entirely dug up and redone every 15 years, costing more than $30,000 per court.

♦ There are three ways players can qualify: 1) rank among the top 104 players who sign up for the Grand Slam; 2) win 3 rounds in the qualifying; and 3) receive a wild card. A total of 128 players get to play in the main draw of each Grand Slam: 104 through ranking, 16 through qualifying, and 8 through wild cards.

♦ The following players never won the French Open, Pete Sampras John McEnroe, Frank Sedgman, John Newcombe, Venus Williams, Stefan Edberg, Boris Becker, Lleyton Hewitt, Jimmy Connors, Louise Brough, Virginia Wade or Martina Hingis.

- Stade Roland Garros which was originally built for the 1924 Olympics but was permanently converted into a tennis facility for this tournament.

- One of the most peculiar customs revolves around a strange ritual involving clay and a broom. According to folklore, if a player sprinkles some clay on their racket during a match, they will eventually become victorious in their quest for a Grand Slam title.

- The 'clay' surface isn't clay—the courts are surfaced with white limestone covered with powdered red brick dust, which gives the courts their ochre color. It is the only Grand Slam event that is played on a red surface. An estimated 44,000kg of crushed red brick are used each year.

- After Serena Williams wore a skin tight cat suit at the 2018 French Open, the French Open declared full body skin tight apparel inappropriate. A new dress code was introduced and in the future all dress must be pre-approved.

- 65,000 Wilson tennis balls are used during the French Open and after use   they are recycled into coatings for sports hall floors.

- Amazon bought exclusive rights to air 10 night-time matches at the 2022 French Open. A new feature at the tournament, thanks to a mammoth $400 million upgrade that included a full rehaul of Philippe Chatrier and the installation of a roof and lights.

- Known officially as the Museum of the French Federation of Tennis, the Tenniseum was designed by the French architect Bruno Moinard and opened in May 2003. It is housed in a former groundsman's cottage, and comprises a multimedia center, media library, and permanent and temporary exhibits dedicated to the history of tennis in general, and the French Open in particular. Permanent exhibits include a display of the French Open perpetual trophies, including La Coupe des Mousquetaires and La Coupe Suzanne Lenglen; a narrative and photographic history of Stade Roland Garros.

- Stade Roland Garros is located at the western side of Paris, at the southern boundary of the Bois de Boulogne in Paris's 16th arrondissement.

- If you cannot get tickets you can watch it for free on big screen TV under the Eiffel Tower.

- The longest clay court match played at Roland Garros was 6 hours and 33 minutes at the 2004 French Open. Fabrice Santoro defeated Arnaud Clement in the 1st round after 2 days: 6-4, 6-3, 6-7 (5), 3-6, 16-14. This was the longest match in history until Wimbledon 2010 where John Isner defeated Nicolas Mahut after 11 hours.

- The first French Open was played in 1891 and was originally played on sand.

- Paris-based research center Memorial de la Shoah owns archive material that confirms Roland Garros was used by the French government as a prison camp or "centre de rassemblement" for political dissidents during a short time in WWII.

- For the first six years it was only open to men, women weren't allowed to take part until 1897.

◆ What is now called the Stade Roland Garros was constructed in 1928 to host France's first defense of the Davis Cup.

◆ In 2022 a new tiebreaker format was agreed to by all of the Grand Slam Tournaments. If the deciding set is tied at six-all, the match is decided in a 10-point format. Should the tiebreaker game be tied at 9-all, whoever scores two straight points wins.

◆ Non-French tennis club members were only allowed to enter the tournament in 1925, when it became the 'French Open'. Before then it was only open to members of French tennis clubs.

◆ Against Felix Mantilla, Safin returned a drop shot with an improbable forehand reply for a winner and promptly bent over and dropped his pants before the amused, if rather stunned, court one crowd at Roland Garros. The 20th seed was docked a point as a penalty for supposedly unsportsmanlike conduct, having been warned earlier for racquet abuse in the four-hour, 39-minute match.

◆ Chris Evert holds the record of the most singles title won in the women's category, from 1974, 1975, 1979, 1980, 1983, 1985, 1986.

◆ Michael Chang became the youngest male singles champion in 1989 at the age of 17 years and 3 months, while Monica Seles at the 16 years and 6 months in 1990 was the youngest women's champion.

◆ Bjorn Borg won the French and Wimbledon back-to-back for three straight years.

- Rafael Nadal was the oldest in the Open era to win the men's singles title, at 36 years and two days of age in 2022.

- Serena Williams is the oldest woman to win the singles title, at 33 years, eight months of age in 2015.

- French Open officials honored Rafael Nadal by erecting a statue made entirely out of steel at the Roland Garros venue.

———

Freed from the thoughts of winning, I instantly play better. I stop thinking, start feeling. My shots become a half-second quicker, my decisions become the product of instinct rather than logic. —ANDRE AGASSI

Wimbledon Championships

The Wimbledon Championships, commonly known simply as Wimbledon, is the oldest tennis tournament in the world and is widely regarded as the most prestigious. It has been held at the All England Club in Wimbledon, London, since 1877 and is played on outdoor grass courts, with retractable roofs over the two main courts since 2019.

Everybody always talks about the pressure of playing at Wimbledon,

how tough it is, but the people watching make it so much easier to play.

—*ANDY MURRAY*

It is the only major still played on grass, the traditional tennis playing surface. Also, it is the only Grand Slam that retains a night-time curfew, though matches can now continue until 11:00 pm under the lights.

The tournament traditionally takes place over two weeks in late June and early July, starting on the last Monday in June and culminating with the Ladies' and Gentlemen's Singles Finals, scheduled for Saturday and Sunday at the end of the second week. A roof was operational over No. 1 Court from 2019, when a number of other improvements were made, including adding cushioned seating, a table and 10 independently operable cameras per court to capture the games.

Wimbledon traditions include a strict all-white dress code for competitors, and royal patronage. Strawberries and cream are traditionally consumed at the tournament. Unlike other tournaments, advertising is minimal and low key from official suppliers such as Slazenger and Rolex. The relationship with Slazenger is the world's longest running sporting sponsorship, providing balls for the tournament since 1902.

Beginning

The All England Lawn Tennis and Croquet Club is a private club founded on 23 July 1868, originally as "The All England Croquet Club". Its first ground was at Nursery Road off Worple Road, Wimbledon.

In 1876, lawn tennis, a game devised by Major Walter Clopton Wingfield a year or so earlier as an outdoor version of real tennis and originally given the name Sphairistikè, was added to the activities of the club. In spring 1877, the club was renamed "The All England Croquet and Lawn Tennis Club" and signaled its change of name by instituting the first Lawn Tennis Championship. A new code of laws, replacing the code administered by the Marylebone Cricket Club, was drawn up for the event. Today's rules are similar except for details such as the height of the net and posts and the distance of the service line from the net.

The inaugural 1877 Wimbledon Championship started on 9 July 1877 and the Gentlemen's Singles was the only event held. Twenty-two men paid a guinea to enter the tournament, which was to be held over five days. Spencer Gore, an old Harrovian rackets player, defeated William Marshall 6–1, 6–2 and 6–4 in

48 minutes. Gore was presented with the silver challenge cup, valued at 25 guineas and donated by the sports magazine The Field, as well as a prize money of 12 guineas. About two hundred spectators paid one shilling each to watch the final.

The lawns at the ground were arranged so that the principal court was in the middle with the others arranged around it, hence the title "Centre Court". The name was retained when the Club moved in 1922 to the present site in Church Road, although no longer a true description of its location. However, in 1980 four new courts were brought into commission on the north side of the ground, which meant the Centre Court was once more correctly described. The opening of the new No. 1 Court in 1997 emphasized the description.

Wimbledon Wind Machine

In 1884, the club added the Ladies' Singles competition and the Gentlemen's Doubles was transferred from the Oxford University Lawn Tennis Club. ladies' doubles and mixed doubles events were added in 1913. The first black player to compete at Wimbledon was Bertrand Milbourne Clark, an amateur from Jamaica, in 1924.

Until 1922, the reigning champion had to play only in the final, against whoever had won through to challenge them. As with the other three Major or Grand Slam events, Wimbledon was contested by top-ranked amateur players; professional players were prohibited from participating. This changed with the advent of the open era in 1968. No British man won the singles event at Wimbledon between Fred Perry in 1936 and Andy Murray in

2013, while no British woman has won since Virginia Wade in 1977, although Annabel Croft and Laura Robson won the Girls' Championship in 1984 and 2008 respectively. The Championship was first televised in 1937.

Though formally called "The Championships, Wimbledon", depending on sources, the event is also known as "The All England Lawn Tennis Championships", the "Wimbledon Championships" or simply "Wimbledon". From 1912 to 1924, the tournament was recognized by the International Lawn Tennis Federation as the "World Grass Court Championships".

- In the period of 1915–1918, no tournament was organized due to World War I.

- During World War II, the tournament was not held in the period 1940–1945.

- In 1946 and 1947 Wimbledon was held before the French Championships and was thus the second Grand Slam tennis event of the year.

The Facilities

Wimbledon is widely considered the world's premier tennis tournament and the priority of the club is to maintain its leadership. To that end a long-term plan was unveiled in 1993, intended to improve the quality of the event for spectators, players, officials, and neighbors. All the changes were completed.

A new retractable roof was built in time for the 2009 championships, marking the first time that rain did not stop play for a lengthy time on Centre Court. The Club tested the new roof at an event called A Centre Court Celebration on Sunday, 17 May 2009, which featured exhibition matches involving Andre Agassi, Steffi Graf, Kim Clijsters, and Tim Henman. The first Championship match to take place under the roof was the completion of the fourth round women's singles match between Dinara Safina and Amélie Mauresmo. The first match to be played in its entirety under the new roof took place between Andy Murray and Stanislas Wawrinka on 29 June 2009. Murray was also involved in the match completed latest in the day at Wimbledon, which ended at 11:02 pm in a victory over Marcos Baghdatis at Centre Court in the third round of the 2012 Championships. The 2012 Gentlemen's Singles Final on 8 July 2012, between Roger Federer and Murray, was the first singles final to be partially played under the roof, which was activated during the third set.

A new 4,000-seat No. 2 Court was built on the site of the old No. 13 Court in time for the 2009 Championships. A new 2,000-seat No. 3 Court was built on the site of the old No. 2 and No. 3 Courts.

In April 2013, Wimbledon unveiled its 'Master Plan' a vision in which to improve the championships over the next 10–15 years.

In a related statement, it was announced that starting at the 2019 Championships, quad wheelchair competitions would become a permanent event.

The Court Surface

The grass plant itself has to survive in this dry soil. Expert research has again shown that a cut height of 8mm (since 1995) is the optimum for present day play and survival.

Courts are sown with one hundred per cent Perennial Ryegrass (since 2001) to improve durability and strengthen the sward to withstand better the increasing wear of the modern game. Its composition is to 100 per cent perennial ryegrass (previously 70 per cent rye/30 per cent creeping red fescue).

Trophies

The Gentlemen's Singles champion is presented with a silver gilt cup 18.5 inches (about 47 cm) in height and 7.5 inches (about 19 cm) in diameter. The trophy has been awarded since 1887 and bears the inscription: "All England Lawn Tennis Club Single Handed Championship of the World". The actual trophy remains the property of the All England Club in their museum, so the champion receives a three-quarter size replica of the Cup bearing the names of all past Champions (height 13.5 inches, 34 cm).

The Ladies' Singles champion is presented with a sterling silver salver commonly known as the "Venus Rosewater Dish", or simply the "Rosewater Dish". The salver, which is 18.75 inches (about 48 cm) in diameter, is decorated with figures from mythology. The actual dish remains the property of the All England Club in their museum, so the champion receives a miniature replica bearing the names of all past Champions. From 1949 to 2006 the replica was 8 inches in diameter, and since 2007 it has been a three-quarter size replica with a diameter of 13.5 inches.

The winner of the Gentlemen's Doubles, Ladies' Doubles, and Mixed Doubles events receive silver cups. A trophy is awarded to each player in the Doubles pair, unlike the other Grand Slam tournaments where the winning Doubles duo shares a single trophy. The Gentlemen's Doubles silver challenge cup was originally from the Oxford University Lawn Tennis Club and donated to the All England Club in 1884. The Ladies' Doubles Trophy, a silver cup and cover known as The Duchess of Kent Challenge Cup, was presented to the All England Club in 1949 by The Duchess of Kent. The Mixed Doubles Trophy is a silver challenge cup and cover presented to the All England Club by the family of two-time Wimbledon doubles winner Sydney Smith.

Do You Know?

Wimbledon

◆ Trophies have been awarded since 1887.

◆ Rufus the hawk is on site at Wimbledon at 5am every day. Pigeons and vermin are scared off by the patrolling hawk.

◆ Rolex has been in unison with Wimbledon ever since 1978, when it became the official timekeeper of The Championships. The company pays $4m a year in a deal that runs until 2022.

◆ The All-England Club has a maze of underground tunnels and rooms hidden from the public. In operation since 1997, the tunnels are the veins of Wimbledon, circulating the lifeblood of the Championships. They help staff get from A to B without crashing into crowds. The tunnels connect many subterranean rooms, such as standard dressing areas to drug-testing rooms. There are two main tunnels: the royal route runs from Centre Court to No. 1 Court, alongside a buggy drive.

◆ There is an archive room, in which hundreds of rackets are stored. Each racket has a tag on it, from names heard long ago to recent greats, often donated and sorted by decade.

◆ There is the library, which stocks about 20,000 books all about tennis. It is open to the public.

◆ A private company performs analysis on each court. The optimum length of grass is 8mm, and the horticulture team gets daily data on this, plus ball hardness and its bounce. The mowers are set at the same height every day,

- There are about fifteen racket-stringers on site during the Championships and they take on requests to re-string up to 450 rackets a day. Players and coaches will pop in with the rackets and make demands on tightness, which varies from player to player. With Babolat electronic stringing machines, the staff set the required tension.

- Most players keep the same set-up on the strings, but they may alter the tension depending on the weather and surface. Players go on court with around 10 rackets, and it is not uncommon to see them rush off court to get their rackets re-strung.

- Nearly 200,000 punnets of strawberries and cream are sold at Wimbledon during the tournament. Now a staple of the Championships, strawberries and cream has been the signature dish since 1877, dating back to King Henry VIII's penchant for snacking on them while watching tennis at Hampton Court Palace.

- Given the amount of Pimm's sold on site during the two weeks — 276,291 glasses at the last Championships with full crowds — one's ear might not twitch at a staff member saying, 'full jug of Pimm's'. But it is said staff have a language of codewords over the radios, and 'full jug of Pimm's' is understood to be code for when an A-list celebrity is on site.

- Last year's final saw the likes of David Beckham, Tom Cruise and the Duchess of Cambridge keep a watching brief from Centre Court. The Royal Box has 80 dark-green Lloyd Loom wicker chairs — the Queen attended in 1957, 1962, 1977 and 2010.

- Around 6,000 staff are taken on for the Championships, including 250 ball boys or girls. They work with 31 local schools, with intense training which starts in January. They have skills and fitness tests and are put into teams of six, with a captain each. Ball girls and boys must walk in silence and cannot speak to players unless spoken to first.

- 53,000 tennis balls are stored at 20°C in two rooms below Centre court and have been supplied by Slazenger since 1902. Before playing each day, twenty tins of balls are delivered to each court.

- Ball-handlers watch each match from a control room, looking for ones that might need new balls.

- 123 balls were used in the 2010 marathon match between John Isner and Nicolas Mahut, which finished 70-68 to Isner in the deciding set.

- Used balls are sold daily at £2.50 per can of three — all proceeds go to local charities.

- The Royals roam freely and are not restricted to their exclusive royal enclosure, one might see Lord Freddie Windsor en route to the Sipsmith Pergola Bar in the company of the Duke of Kent. Or even the Duchess of Cambridge slipping casually into Court 9 to witness an up-and-coming British wildcard embark on Wimbledon glory.

- The All England Club maintains what it calls "The List"—an exhaustive and comprehensive tally of everything staff members suggest they can do better.

With over 1,000 things added to the list in a process that starts immediately after the tournament has finished, you may think some of the items get hastily ignored. This is not the case, as every item on the list gets discussed and addressed before the next Championships. Improvements can range from huge renovations that take years, or trivial matters such as a squeaky chair on a certain court, or a signage post needing a new paint job.

♦ For 50 weeks a year Centre Court remains out of bounds for players, and experiences only the tender care of the ground staff team. But with the grass perfected over the course of four seasons, the first players to experience a match on it this year will not be defending men's champion Novak Djokovic and his opponent Philip Kohlschreiber but a select group of AELTC members. Every year, on the Saturday before the tournament, a group of female players (lighter than their male counterparts and less likely to inadvertently cause any damage to the court) step out to test that the grass is pinpoint perfect before the players take center stage on Monday.

♦ The players bow to the King and the Queen when they visit.

♦ Wimbledon remains one of the only major sporting events in the UK where spectators can buy premium tickets on the day of the event. To do this, however, almost invariably requires spending the night in The Queue or waiting all day in line. Those who do so often bring tents, folding chairs, games, and food with them. Each person receives a card indicating their place in the queue, and there is no way to hold a place for anyone else.

◆ There are no advertisements at the All-England Club.

◆ In 2012, the All England Club hosted the Summer Olympic Games and became the first Olympic grass court tournament since tennis was reintroduced as an Olympic sport and the first to be held at a Grand Slam venue in the Open era.

◆ The dress code is strictly enforced. It is an all-white dress code for competitors. Since the last update in 2014, the Wimbledon dress code now forbids any non-white clothing that could at any time become visible during play due to movement, lighting, or perspiration.

◆ Wimbledon is relaxing its requirement for all-white clothing to allow female players to wear colored undershorts beginning in 2023. Wimbledon's famously strict rules requiring all-white clothing for its players now comes with an exception: female players can wear dark-colored undershorts beneath their skirts or shorts.

◆ Kate Middleton is now the Patron of the All-England Club. Queen Elizabeth resigned from the post in 2016 after her 90th birthday — she had been the Patron since 1952, according to The Wimbledon Compendium 2019, an encyclopedia published by the All England Club — handing off the role to her grandson's wife. The Duchess has served in this role since the 2017 tournament.

◆ There is no official Wimbledon dress code for spectators beyond a few forbidden items: no torn jeans, running vests, dirty sneakers, or sport shorts. Though this is all that will be formally enforced, visitors to Centre Court are still expected to dress up.

- In all matches used balls will be replaced by new balls at the conclusion of the first seven games and thereafter at the conclusion of every ninth game. Subject to availability, used tennis balls will be sold at the Southern Village store.

- In 1995, during a match between Tim Henman and Jeremy Bates, a ball girl fainted on court due to heat exhaustion. The incident prompted officials to review their policies for ball kids working in hot weather.

- During the 2013 championships, a swarm of flying ants descended upon the courts causing players to swat at them during matches.

- In 2017, during a match between Jo-Wilfried Tsonga and Simone Bolelli, a spectator dressed in all white walked onto Court One mid-match and began playing tennis with himself using an old wooden racket before being escorted off by security.

- There are forty-two grass courts at Wimbledon.

- The name of the Centre Court is the No. 1 Court, and it was built in 1922.

- In 1907, the Prince of Wales and Princess Mary (who would soon become King George V and Queen Mary) attended the Wimbledon Championships. This marked the first time the royal family had a connection with the tournament.

The US Open Tennis Championships

The US Open Tennis Championships is a hardcourt tennis tournament held annually in Queens, New York. Since 1987, the US Open has been chronologically the fourth and final Grand Slam tournament of the year. The US Open starts on the last Monday of August and continues for two weeks, with the middle weekend coinciding with the US Labor Day holiday. The tournament is of one of the oldest tennis championships in the world, originally known as the U.S. National Championship, for which men's singles and men's doubles were first played in August 1881.

"Being an American playing at the US Open is incredible. I think this atmosphere, out of all the Slams, is pretty unmatched. I think this is, like, the peak of the peak."—SLOANE STEPHEN

The tournament consists of five primary championships: men's and women's singles, men's and women's doubles, and mixed doubles. The tournament also includes events for senior, junior, and wheelchair players. Since 1978, the tournament has been played on acrylic hardcourts at the USTA Billie Jean King National Tennis Center in Flushing Meadows–Corona Park, Queens, New York City. The US Open is owned and organized by the United States Tennis Association (USTA), a non-profit organization. Revenue from ticket sales, sponsorships, and television contracts is used to develop tennis in the United States.

The tournament was first held in August 1881 on grass courts at the Newport Casino in Newport, Rhode Island, which is now home to the International Tennis Hall of Fame. That year, only clubs that were members of the United States National Lawn Tennis Association (USNLTA) were permitted to enter.

Flushing Meadows–Corona Park, Queens, New York City

In the first years of the U.S. National Championship, only men competed, and the tournament was known as the U.S. National Singles Championships for Men. In September 1887, six years after the men's nationals were first held, the first U.S. Women's National Singles Championship was held at the Philadelphia Cricket Club.

The women's tournament used a challenge system from 1888 through 1918, except in 1917. Between 1890 and 1906, sectional tournaments were held in the east and the west of the country to determine the best two doubles teams, which competed in a play-off for the right to compete against the defending champions in the challenge round.

The 1888 and the 1889 men's doubles events were played at the Staten Island Cricket Club in Livingston, Staten Island, New York. In the 1893 Championship, the men's doubles event was played at the St. George Cricket Club in Chicago.[8][9][10] In 1892, the

US Mixed Doubles Championship was introduced and in 1899 the US Women's National Doubles Championship.

In August 1915, the men's singles tournament was held in the West Side Tennis Club, Forest Hills in New York City for the first time while the women's tournament was held in Philadelphia Cricket Club in Chestnut Hill, Philadelphia (the women's singles event was not moved until 1921). From 1917 to 1933, the men's doubles event was held in Longwood Cricket Club in Chestnut Hill, Massachusetts. From 1934 to 1941 and 1941 to 1967, both men's and women's doubles events were held in Longwood Cricket Club.

From 1921 through 1923, the men's singles tournament was played at the Germantown Cricket Club in Philadelphia. It returned to the West Side Tennis Club in 1924 following completion of the 14,000-seat Forest Hills Stadium.

The open era began in 1968 when professional tennis players were allowed to compete for the first time at the Grand Slam tournament held at the West Side Tennis Club. The previous U.S. National Championships had been limited to amateur players. Except for mixed doubles, all events at the 1968 national tournament were open to professionals. That year, ninety-six men and 63 women entered, and prize money totaled $100,000. In 1970, the US Open became

Emily Murphy and Kelly Quinlan two graduates of Grandpa's Tennis Academy at the US Open

the first Grand Slam tournament to use a tiebreaker to decide a set that reached a 6–6 score in games. system.] In 1973, the US Open became the first Grand Slam tournament to award equal prize money to men and women, with that year's singles champions, John Newcombe and Margaret Court, receiving $25,000 each.

From 1975, following complaints about the surface and its impact on the ball's bounce, the tournament played on clay courts instead of grass. This was also an experiment to make it more "TV friendly". The addition of floodlights allowed matches to be played at night.

In 1978, the tournament moved from the West Side Tennis Club to the larger and newly constructed USTA National Tennis Center in Flushing Meadows, Queens. The tournament's court surface also switched from clay to hard.

During the 2006 US Open, the complex was renamed to "USTA Billie Jean King National Tennis Center" in honor of Billie Jean King, a four-time US Open singles champion and women's tennis pioneer.

From 1984 through 2015, the US Open deviated from traditional scheduling practices for tennis tournaments with a concept that came to be known as "Super Saturday": the women's and men's finals were played on the final Saturday and Sunday of the tournament respectively, and their respective semifinals were held one day prior. The women's final was originally held in between the two men's semifinal matches; in 2001, the women's final was moved to the evening so it could be played on primetime television, citing a major growth in popularity for women's tennis among viewers. This scheduling pattern helped to encourage television viewership, but proved divisive among players because it only gave them less than a day's rest between their semifinals and championship match.

Facilities

The grounds of the US Open have twenty-two outdoor courts (plus twelve practice courts just outside the East Gate) consisting of four "show courts" (Arthur Ashe Stadium, Louis Armstrong Stadium, the Grandstand, and Court 17), 13 field courts, and 5 practice courts.

The main court is the 23,771-seat Arthur Ashe Stadium, which opened in 1997. A US$180 million retractable roof was added in 2016. The stadium is named after Arthur Ashe, who won the men's singles title at the inaugural US Open in 1968, the Australian Open in 1970, and Wimbledon in 1975 and who was inducted into the International Tennis Hall of Fame in 1985. The next largest court is the 14,061-seat Louis Armstrong Stadium, which cost US$200 million to build and opened in 2018. The 6,400-seat lower tier of this stadium is separately ticketed, reserved seating while the 7,661-seat upper tier is general admission and not separately ticketed. The third largest court is the 8,125-seat Grandstand in the southwest corner of the grounds, which opened in 2016. Court 17 in the southeast corner of the grounds is the fourth largest stadium. It opened with temporary seating in 2011 and received its permanent seating the following year. It has a seating capacity of 2,800, all of which is general admission and not separately ticketed. It is nicknamed "The Pit", partly because the playing surface is sunk 8 feet into the ground.

The Court Surface

From 1978 to 2019, the US Open was played on a hardcourt surface called Pro DecoTurf. It is a multi-layer cushioned surface and classified by the International Tennis Federation as medium-fast. Each August before the start of the tournament, the courts are resurfaced.[47] In March 2020, the USTA announced that Laykold would become the new court surface supplier beginning with the 2020 tournament.

Since 2005, all US Open and US Open Series tennis courts have been painted a shade of blue (trademarked as "US Open Blue") inside the lines to make it easier for players, spectators, and television viewers to see the ball. The area outside the lines is still painted "US Open Green".

US Open; Arthur Ashe Stadium; Flushing Meadows–Corona Park in Queens, NYC

Trophies

The US Open presents permanent trophies that remain at the venue, in common with the other Grand Slam events. They are impressive sterling silver creations, bearing the name of the US Lawn Tennis Association, and engraved with the names of the previous winners.

All trophy work at the US Open since 1987 has been undertaken by iconic jewelers Tiffany & Co, as immortalized on film by Audrey Hepburn. The men's trophy weighs a fairly hefty ten pounds, so it is not ideal for an exhausted player to wield after a long final. Although the US Open follows Wimbledon and Roland Garros in issuing replica trophies to the winners, it differs by making them the same size as the originals.

DO YOU KNOW?

The US Open

◆ Traditionally, the fourth and final Grand Slam of the year, the U.S. Open is scheduled on the last Monday of August and goes until the second Sunday of September.

◆ Since 2005, all US Open and US Open Series tennis courts have been painted a shade of blue (trademarked as "US Open Blue") inside the lines to make it easier for players, spectators, and television viewers to see the ball. The area outside the lines is still painted "US Open Green".

◆ The USTA Billie Jean King National Tennis Center is located in Flushing Meadows–Corona Park in New York City. The facility is home to 22 hard courts, including 3 show courts: Arthur Ashe Stadium, Louis Armstrong Stadium, and Grandstand.

◆ In 1975, the U.S. Open became the first Grand Slam tournament to feature night matches.

◆ In 2001, Venus and Serena Williams became the first sisters to meet in a grand slam final at the US Open. The match lasted 69 minutes, with Venus winning 6-2, 6-4.

◆ Tennis became the first sport, and the U.S. Open became the first Grand Slam to offer equal prize money to men and women. This all started in 1973 when Billie Jean King threatened to boycott the event.

DO YOU KNOW
The US Open

- Arthur Ashe was the only African American male to win the US Open and he won in 1968.

- The Arthur Ashe stadium was completed in 1997 and included a roof in 2016. The stadium is the largest tennis stadium in the world, seating 23,771 people.

- The youngest men's singles champion in U.S. Open history is Pete Sampras, who was 19 years, 28 days old when he won the title in 1990, defeating Andre Agassi in straight sets.

- The youngest women's singles champion is Tracy Austin at the 1979 U.S. Open where she beat Chris Evert to win the title at the age of 16 years and eight months.

- The 2006 US Open became the first of the majors to allow players to challenge line calls via the Hawk-Eye system.

- The Honey Deuce is known as the official cocktail of the U.S. Open. The mixture includes Grey Goose Vodka, lemonade, Chambord liqueur and ice garnished with four honeydew melon balls.

- Jimmy Connors, Pete Sampras, and Roger Federer are tied with five U.S. Open men's singles titles—the most in the Open Era. Both Chris Evert and Serena Williams have the most women's singles titles with six each.

- In 2015, during a women's singles match, a moth flew into Serena Williams' ear causing her to panic and seek medical attention mid-match. Play was suspended as medics attended to her ear before she eventually returned and won the match.

◈ Top of Form—The new roof at this year's opening is made up of two 1-million-pound plates that were installed at a cost of $100 million. It takes 5.5 minutes to close.

◈ Finally, in 2009 during a men's singles match between Andy Roddick and Janko Tipsarevic, there was an unusual noise coming from within or near Roddick's bag. It turned out that he had accidentally sat on his phone which then called his wife's number resulting in some awkward moments!

◈ The U.S.T.A. had consulted meteorologists who said the Open coincided with traditionally dry weeks, so officials had decided against a retractable roof.

◈ Best value is during the qualifying tournament the week before the Opening Day where you can see up close the best up and coming tennis players in the world. They compete for the final 32 spots (16 for men and 16 for women). Another bonus is seeing the top players in the world on the practice courts. All for free.

◈ For practices on Ashe, you need to register for a Fan Access Pass to access practices in Ashe.

◈ The open era began in 1968 when professional tennis players were allowed to compete for the first time at the Grand Slam tournament held at the West Side Tennis Club. The previous U.S. National Championships had been limited to amateur players. Except for mixed doubles, all events at the 1968 national tournament were open to professionals. That year, ninety-six men and sixty-three women entered, and prize money totaled $100,000.

◆ Althea Gibson died in 2003 at the age of seventy-six. In August 2019, the U.S. Tennis Association honored her with a statue at the Billie Jean King National Tennis Center, the home of the U.S. Open.

◆ Celebrities like Taylor Swift, Katie Holmes, Tom Cruise, Zac Efron, Maria Sharapova, Justin Bieber, Mike Tyson, CC Sabathia, Trevor Noah, Jay Z, Beyonce Knowles-Carter, Jennifer Lopez, Alex Rodriguez, Jamie Foxx, Jon Bon Jovi, Matthew Perry, Andy Cohen, Ben Stiller, Bella Hadid, Gayle King, Aaron Judge, Anne Hathaway, Naomi Watts, Spike Lee, LeBron James, Jerry Seinfeld, Anna Wintour, Tiger Woods, Hugh Jackman, and Derek Jeter and many more, have made an appearance at various US Open matches.

◆ The US Open is known for its unique fan experiences, such as the Arthur Ashe Kids' Day, which features interactive activities for children, and the US Open Fan Week, where fans can watch qualifying matches and attend player practices for free.

◆ The US Open is broadcasted in over 200 countries around the world, making it one of the most widely watched tennis tournaments.

◆ 128 male and female players compete for the final 32 spots (16 each for men and women) in the singles draws.

Other Major Tournaments

*ATP Tour Masters 1000 · ATP Tour 500
WTA Tour Premier*

In addition to the four Grand Slam tournaments, there are several other major tournaments in tennis. These include the ATP Tour Masters 1000, the ATP Tour 500, and the WTA Tour Premier events. The Masters 1000 tournaments are considered the second most prestigious events in men's tennis, after the Grand Slams. They are held on three surfaces: hard, clay and indoor. The ATP Tour 500 and the WTA Tour Premier events are considered the third most prestigious tournaments in their respective tours.

There are also several team events in tennis, including the Davis Cup (men's) and the Fed Cup (women's), which feature teams representing different countries competing against each other. The ATP Cup and Laver Cup are also team events, but they are not officially recognized by ITF.

Additionally, there are many lower-level tournaments, such as the ITF Men's and Women's Circuit, which give up-and-coming players a chance to gain experience and rankings points.

BNP PARIBAS OPEN

The BNP Paribas Open is an annual tennis tournament held in Indian Wells, California. The tournament is hosted at the Indian Wells Tennis Garden, which features 29 courts and can hold up to 16,100 spectators.

The event is one of the biggest and most prestigious tournaments in the tennis world, attracting the top men's and women's players from around the globe. The tournament is a part of the ATP World Tour Masters 1000 series and the WTA Premier Mandatory series, which are two of the highest categories in the professional tennis tour.

The BNP Paribas Open has a rich history dating back to 1976 when it was first held. The first tournament was known as the American Airlines Tennis Games and only featured a men's singles event. Nevertheless, the event has grown significantly over the years, with the addition of a women's singles event in 1989, as well as men's and women's doubles competitions.

James Henry Van Alen Iii was an American tennis official and former player. He was best known for his influence of tennis, especially for the tiebreak and for being the founder and primary benefactor of the International Tennis Hall of Fame at the Newport Casino.

Some of the greatest tennis players of all time have competed at the BNP Paribas Open, including Roger Federer, Rafael Nadal, Novak Djokovic, Serena Williams, and Steffi Graf. The tournament has also seen some memorable matches, with the longest men's singles match on record taking place in 2012 between John Isner and Nicolas Mahut, which lasted for 11 hours and 5 minutes.

The BNP Paribas Open offers a total prize money of $17.7 million, making it one of the richest tournaments on the tennis calendar. The tournament has also been known to pioneer new technologies in tennis, such as the Hawk-Eye system and the Electronic Line Calling system.

Overall, the BNP Paribas Open is an important event in the tennis world, known for its high standards and top-quality play. Fans and players alike look forward to this tournament every year as it offers a unique and memorable experience.

DAVIS CUP

The Davis Cup is an annual international tennis tournament contested by teams from competing nations across the world. It is organized and governed by the International Tennis Federation (ITF). The event was first held in 1900, making it the world's longest-running team competition in sport.

The Davis Cup consists of a series of men's singles and doubles matches played between teams from different countries over a period of one week. Each tie is held at a predetermined venue, with one of the participating countries serving as the host nation. These countries must pay their own expenses for hosting the tournament, including providing accommodation and practice facilities for players and officials.

The competition is divided into four separate stages: World Group, Regional Zone Groups I & II, Qualifying Rounds, and Playoff Round. Throughout each stage, teams are eliminated until two remain to compete in the final round—known as 'The Final'—at which point one nation will become declared champion of that year's Davis Cup.

Each season culminates in The Final where either two or three day of competition will take place to determine the winner—depending on whether it is a best-of-three or best-of-five format match. In addition to these head-to-head matches between nations, The Final also includes an awards ceremony where players receive medals for their performance throughout the tournament and other relevant acknowledgements are made.

The Davis Cup teams are comprised of four players representing their country. Each team is allowed to field a new line-up each round, selecting from a squad of up to five players. The team's captain is also allowed to designate two additional non-playing captains, who will act as support and advice during the matches.

To qualify for the tournament, countries must go through the qualifying rounds, where they need to win at least two matches. After reaching the World Group stage, teams are divided into eight groups of three or four countries. Winners from these groups move on to compete in the knockout stages, before eventually competing in 'The Final' for the Davis Cup trophy.

Over time, many of tennis' greatest stars have represented their countries in The Davis Cup competition, with some becoming huge icons throughout its long history—such as Roger Federer (Switzerland), Rafael Nadal (Spain) and Novak Djokovic (Serbia). In addition to these world-renowned players, many lesser-known names have played a vital role in team success over the years and contributed significantly to their nation's involvement in The Davis Cup.

The United States of America has won the most Davis Cup championships, having lifted the trophy a total of thirty-two times. Founded in 1900 and based in London, the Davis Cup is an international tennis tournament contested by teams from across the world in a series of men's singles and doubles matches over a period of one week each year.

Since its inception, the United States team has dominated the competition, winning their first title in 1920 and going on to add a further thirty-one victories over the years. Their most recent championship win came in 2007 when they beat Russia 4–1 in Moscow. The US team also holds the record for most consecutive titles with seven between 1950-1957.

In second place is Australia who have been crowned champions twenty-eight times since 1907—making them one of only two countries to lift the trophy outside North America (the other being the Czech Republic). They recorded their most successful streak between 1939-1950 where they won seven consecutive titles. Other nations to have achieved significant success in The Davis Cup include Sweden, France, and Britain—who have all won multiple championships throughout its history.

THE BILLIE JEAN CUP

The Billie Jean King Cup (or the BJK Cup) is the premier inter-national team competition in women's tennis, launched as the Federation Cup in 1963 to celebrate the 50th anniversary of the International Tennis Federation (ITF). The name was changed to the Fed Cup in 1995, and changed again in September 2020 in honor of former World No. 1 Billie Jean King. The Billie Jean King Cup is the world's largest annual women's international team sports competition in terms of the number of nations that compete. The current Chairperson is Katrina Adams.

The Czech Republic dominated the BJK Cup in the 2010s, winning six of ten competitions in the decade. The men's equivalent of the Billie Jean King Cup is the Davis Cup, and the Czech

Republic, Australia, Russia and the United States are the only countries to have held both Cups at the same time.

There are thousands of tournaments all over the world, the above are among the best known along with the Grand Slams. Played by professionals and amateurs, each competing to the best of their abilities. All a tribute to the game of tennis.

THE LAVER CUP

The Laver Cup is a new event in tennis, having only been established in 2017. It was named after legendary Australian tennis player, Rod Laver, and is an annual international men's team competition featuring players from Europe and the rest of the world.

The idea of the Laver Cup was conceived by Roger Federer, who envisioned a format that would enable the sport's top players to compete against each other in a fun, yet competitive atmosphere. The event takes place over three days and consists of both singles and doubles matches, with each team aiming to reach 13 points to secure victory.

The first Laver Cup was held in Prague, Czech Republic, and was won by Team Europe, led by Federer and his long-time rival, Rafael Nadal. In subsequent years, the event has been held in Chicago, Geneva, and Boston, with Team Europe emerging as champions each time.

One unique aspect of the Laver Cup is the team dynamic, with players from different countries coming together to compete as one unit. It has also provided an opportunity for younger players to gain experience playing alongside some of the sport's biggest stars.

Each team comprises of six players, with four earning direct qualification due to their ATP ranking, and two receiving Captain's picks. Matches are played in a best-of-three sets format, with the final set played as a 10-point tiebreaker, ensuring that the competition remains tight and exciting for spectators.

While the Laver Cup is not officially recognized by the ATP or WTA tours, it has quickly become one of the most highly anticipated events on the tennis calendar. With its exciting format, passionate crowds, and top-notch talent, it is sure to remain a fixture in the sport for years to come.

With each passing year, it continues to wow tennis enthusiasts and cement its position as a must-see spectacle on the tennis calendar.

"Most players who play tennis love the game. But I think you also have to respect it. You want to do everything you can in your power to do your best. And for me, I know I get insane guilt if I go home at the end of the day and don't feel I've done everything I can. If I know I could have done something better, I have this uneasy feeling."—ANDY RODDICK

Do You Know?

Major Tournaments

◆ Roger Federer's management company, TEAM8, Brazilian businessman and former Davis Cup player Jorge Paulo Lemann, and Tennis Australia partnered to create the Laver Cup.

◆ Roger Federer was inspired to create a tennis team tournament based on the biennial Ryder Cup golf tournament, which features the best golfers from the United States playing against the best golfers from Europe.

◆ Laver Cup differs as it is purely an invitational event based on past historical performances; selection of (and the playing agreement with) the tournament participants are not automatically based from the highest ranked players of the recent ATP Tour world rankings.

◆ Former rivals Björn Borg of Sweden (Team Europe) and John McEnroe of the United States (Team World) were announced to serve as captains for at least the first three editions.

◆ After the 2019 edition, they announced that they will reprise their roles as team captains for a fourth straight edition.

"All you have to do is to hit this small ball with power, spin and accuracy!—BOB GAMACHE

"I enjoyed the position I was in as a tennis player. I was to blame when I lost. I was to blame when I won. And I really like that, because I played soccer a lot too, and I couldn't stand it when I had to blame it on the goalkeeper."—
ROGER FEDERER

The Women's Tennis Association

The Women's Tennis Association (WTA) is the principal governing body of professional women's tennis. It was founded in 1973 by Billie Jean King and her associate, Gladys Heldman, and it is headquartered in St. Petersburg, Florida. The mission of the WTA is to promote the game of tennis around the world, as well as to support and develop female tennis players who compete at all levels and ages.

The WTA sanctions tournaments on four main levels: Premier Tournaments, International Series Events, Fed/Davis Cup Events, and ITF Junior Tournaments. The organization also runs several developmental tours for young professionals looking to hone their skills before entering the professional ranks: Pro-Circuit, Future Stars Circuit and Rising Stars Invitationals.

In addition to providing a platform for professional players' competitions, the WTA also offers a wide range of educational programs aimed at inspiring young tennis fans and educating them about the sport. These initiatives include introducing kids to tennis through its 'Rising Stars' program; connecting future generations with the history of tennis

Clinics with top coaches; hosting 'Kids Day' events throughout North America

through its Hall of Fame; creating educational resources such as magazines, websites and digital games; running clinics with top coaches; hosting 'Kids Day' events throughout North America; and providing free tickets for students at select events across Europe.

As well as promoting women's professional tennis by organizing events throughout the year in various locations around the globe—from Auckland to San Jose—the WTA runs a comprehensive website which provides news coverage from all leading tournaments taking place throughout the world.

The WTA is committed to fostering a global community that celebrates tennis as a sport and celebrates its athletes as role models for younger generations. All these efforts have helped make women's professional tennis more popular than ever before.

Do You Know?

....

The Women's Tennis Association

◆ In the past 10 years women tennis players make up more than 80 per cent of the top women athlete earners.

◆ Once the first Virginia Slims Tournament was announced the participants were suspended from the ITA but it was soon revoked.

◆ The Virginia Slims slogan "You've come a long way baby" became an iconic phrase of the era and was used to promote women's rights and equality in sport.

◆ WTA Charities, the philanthropic arm of the WTA and WTA Tour title sponsor Hologic have renewed their financial support for researchers and nonprofits dedicated to fighting cancers that affect women through the ACEing Cancer campaign. Hologic makes a donation to the campaign for every ace served during singles competition at WTA 1000 and WTA 500 tournaments in 2023.

◆ The WTA rankings are updated every Monday and are based on a rolling 52-week period. This means that points earned in tournaments from the previous year are gradually replaced by points earned in more recent tournaments.

◆ The WTA operates on a global scale and hosts tournaments on every continent except Antarctica.

Tennis Trivia

1.   Who are these two players.

JOHN MCENROE AND ARTHUR ASHE

2.   Who won the most matches between Jimmy Connors and John McEnroe?

JOHN MCENROE 20 TO 14

3.   Who is this player? Identify this player and his country of origin.

ION TIRIAC OF ROMANIA

4.   What record does Steffi Graf still hold today?

377 WEEKS RANKED AS THE NUMBER 1 FEMALE PLAYER IN THE WORLD.

5.   What are clay courts composed of?

CLAY COURTS ARE MADE OF CRUSHED STONE, BRICK, SHALE, OR OTHER UNBOUND MINERAL AGGREGATE.

6.   Why is Stan Smith well known outside of tennis?

HE IS BEST KNOWN TO NON-TENNIS PLAYERS AS THE NAMESAKE OF A POPULAR BRAND OF TENNIS SHOES.

7.   What was unique about Flavia Pennetta's win at the US Open in 2015?

SHE BEAT HER CHILDHOOD FRIEND.

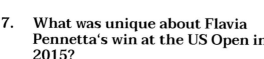

8. In 2003 what titles did Kim Clijsters hold simultaneously?

NO1 IN WOMEN'S SINGLES AND DOUBLES.

9. In which year was the first Wimbledon championship held?

1877

10. Who holds both records for being ranked number 1 by ATP for most consecutive week?

NOVAK DJOKOVIC HAS SPENT THE MOST WEEKS AS WORLD NO. 1, A RECORD TOTAL 380 WEEKS.

11. When did Roger Federer win his lone French Open title?

2009

12. Who won the most Grand Slam singles titles in men's professional tennis?

RAFAEL NADAL AND NOVAK DJOKOVIC EACH HAVE WON TWENTY-TWO.

13. Who did Steffi Graf lose to in her first professional tournament?

SHE LOST HER FIRST-ROUND MATCH 6–4, 6–0 TO TRACY AUSTIN, A TWO-TIME US OPEN CHAMPION AND FORMER WORLD NO. 1 PLAYER.

14. Who was the last British male to win a Grand Slam tournament singles title before Andy Murray's success at 2012 US Open and 2013 Wimbledon Championships?

FRED PERRY

15. How many times has Rafael Nadal won at Roland Garros (the French Open)?

FOURTEEN

16. What country has won the most Olympic gold medals in tennis?

TWENTY UNITED STATES

17. Where was Steffi Graf born, and when did she turn professional in tennis?

GERMANY AGE 13

18. Which female player has won more grand slams than any other women on tour today?

SERENA WILLIAMS

19. What country does Martina Navratilova come from?

CZECHOSLOVAKIA

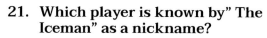

20. What is the total number of Grand Slam tournaments?

FOUR

21. Which player is known by" The Iceman" as a nickname?

ROGER FEDERER

22. Who was the first non-European player to win Wimbledon?

DON BUDGE 1935

23. What country does Maria Sharapova come from?

RUSSIA

24. How best to describe Ken Rosewall's serve?

SOFT BUT ACCURATE.

25. How many consecutive years did Björn Borg win Wimbledon between 1976 and 1981?

FIVE TIMES 1976-1980

26. What is the largest stadium used for a Grand Slam tennis tournament?

US OPEN ARTHUR ASHE STADIUM SEATING CAPACITY 20,771

27. When did Martina Navratilova retire?

AFTER WINNING THE MIXED DOUBLES AT THE U.S. OPEN IN 2006, SHE RETIRED FROM COMPETITIVE PLAY.

28. How often do professional players have their racquet re-strung?

EVERY FEW GAMES—NONPROFESSIONALS BETWEEN ONE MONTH AND A YEAR AND SOME AMATEURS NEVER

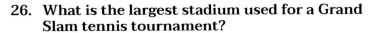

29. Who holds the record for most singles titles by a woman in Grand Slams history?

MARGARET COURT — 24 GRAND SLAM SINGLES TITLES

30. Where was the first Australian Open held in 1905?

MELBOURNE CRICKET CLUB

31. In what year was Carlos Alcaraz Garfia born?

2003

32. What type of gas inside a pressurized tennis ball?

INACTIVE OR INERT NITROGEN GAS

33. What was the longest match ever played at Wimbledon

IN 2019, THE LONGEST EVER WIMBLEDON MATCH WAS PLAYED BETWEEN KEVIN ANDERSON AND JOHN ISNER, LASTING 6 HOURS AND 36 MINUTES.

34. Who calls out the score in a professional tennis match?

THE CHAIR UMPIRE.

35. What is the name for doubles match in which each team has a male and a female player?

MIXED DOUBLES

36. When a server's feet leave the ground while serving—is that a fault?

NO

37. What is the biggest non-Grand Slam tournament?

INDIAN WELLS IN ARIZONA

38. TheRoyal Box has been used for the entertainment of friends and guests of Wimbledon since 1922. How many seats are in the Royal Box?

74

39. Can you serve underhand in tennis?

WHILE SERVING UNDERHAND IS NOT AS COMMON AS SERVING OVERHAND, IT IS COMPLETELY WITHIN THE RULES OF TENNIS.

40. There is only one player who has won the Australian Open on grass and hard surface. Who was that player?

MATS WILANDER

41. What type of material are tennis balls made out of?

TENNIS BALLS ARE TYPICALLY MADE OUT OF A PRESSURIZED RUBBER CORE THAT IS COVERED WITH FELT.

42. What is the standard tension range for tennis racket strings?

THE STANDARD TENSION RANGE FOR TENNIS RACKET STRINGS IS TYPICALLY BETWEEN 50 TO 70 POUNDS.

43. What is the difference between a tennis shoe and a regular athletic shoe?

TENNIS SHOES TYPICALLY HAVE A FLATTER SOLE AND PROVIDE MORE LATERAL SUPPORT SINCE TENNIS INVOLVES A LOT OF QUICK SIDEWAYS MOVEMENTS.

44. Where is the deuce line on a tennis court?

THERE IS NO DEUCE LINE.

45. What is the purpose of the vibration dampener on a tennis racket?

THE VIBRATION DAMPENER ON A TENNIS RACKET HELPS REDUCE THE AMOUNT OF SHOCK AND VIBRATION FELT BY THE PLAYER'S ARM WHEN HITTING THE BALL.

46. What is the purpose of hitting a slice shot in tennis?

TO KEEP THE BALL LOW AND CAUSE IT TO SPIN AWAY FROM THE OPPONENT, MAKING IT DIFFICULT TO RETURN WITH POWER.

47. Myth or Fact: A tennis player can be penalized for grunting too loudly while playing?

FACT. SOME TENNIS PLAYERS, SUCH AS MARIA SHARAPOVA AND VICTORIA AZARENKA, HAVE BEEN PENALIZED BY UMPIRES FOR EXCESSIVE GRUNTING.

"I love my life. I commentate for Eurosport, so you could say I've reached the final of every grand slam since 2002 when I started that. I love what I do, and I love playing tennis with amateurs, regular guys, helping to teach them to enjoy tennis more."—MATS WILANDER.

More About Tennis

What Professional Tennis Players Know
That Amateur Players Do Not

There is no doubt that the skills and knowledge of professional tennis players sets them apart from amateur players. From using the right techniques, strategies, and equipment to mastering the mental aspect of tennis, professionals have a distinct advantage over amateur players.

One of the most important things that pros know about tennis is shot placement. Learning to consistently hit an accurate shot in any given situation can mean the difference between winning and losing a match. Professional players use their experience on the court to hone their ability to place shots strategically and catch their opponents off-guard when needed.

In addition, professionals understand how to read their opponents' body language and tactics which can give them an edge during a match. They are also able to adjust their own game plans quickly in response to what they observe on court—something that takes time for amateurs to learn.

Mentally, professional players must be able to stay focused while they play multiple games or matches back-to-back during long events. They understand the importance of visualizing success prior to each match and having a positive attitude on court regardless of the scoreline or circumstances. Mental toughness is key in tennis because there will be moments when a player needs to push themselves hard even when tired or feeling overwhelmed by their opponent's performance.

So, if you want to take your game up a notch—learning what professional tennis players know about technique, tactics and fitness will surely help point you in the right direction!

Unsung Heroes of Tournament Play

The unsung heroes of modern tennis are the ball boys and girls who work long hours in hot conditions to make sure that players have the perfect playing surface during a match. Though they may seem like a small part of the game, their efforts are invaluable in allowing professional players to reach peak performance. They often arrive hours before the match starts, working hard to mark out courts, place lines and mop up any spills. During a match, they are responsible for keeping track of balls and ensuring that play is not disrupted by debris or other distractions on court.

Ball kids must have excellent agility and coordination skills so they can quickly retrieve balls from across the court and deliver them directly to the player without impacting their momentum or concentration. In addition, it requires excellent communication skills as ball boys and girls need to be able to interact with referees and respond promptly to requests from players or coaches. The job also requires a good level of discipline as ball kids must remain calm under pressure and maintain absolute focus throughout long matches.

In spite of their important contributions, ball kids often go unrecognized by fans and commentators alike—they may be briefly mentioned during pauses in play but otherwise their efforts go unnoticed. Nevertheless, these unsung heroes continue to use their agility, coordination, and communication skills to help ensure that professional matches run smoot ily.

The unsung heroes of modern tennis are the ball boys and girls who work diligently throughout a match to ensure that players have the perfect playing surface. They arrive hours ahead of the match to mark out courts, place lines and mop up any spills. During a match, they must quickly retrieve balls from across the court and deliver them directly to the player, while also remaining calm under pressure and communicating with referees.

These individuals often go unrecognized by fans, but their efforts are invaluable in allowing professional players to reach peak performance. Ball kids must have excellent agility and coordination skills, as well as an ability to remain focused during long matches. In addition, they need strong communication skills in order to interact with referees and respond promptly to requests from players or coaches.

It is a physically demanding job requiring many hours of standing in hot conditions—yet these unsung heroes do it all with dedication, ensuring that professional matches run smoothly. Without them, games would be disrupted by debris or other distractions on court; thus their contribution is essential for the progression of this great sport.

At grand slam tournaments, ball boys and girls are usually paid minimum wage for their services. However, in some cases they may receive additional compensation depending on the tournament and regulations in place. For instance, for the US Open 2020, ball kids were paid an hourly rate of $12.50 as well as receiving daily meal allowances, a souvenir gift bag, and complimentary tickets to matches. Furthermore, all ball kids at the US Open are given a uniform consisting of clothing items such as t-shirts and shorts.

In Australia, ball kids at the Australian Open have received free flights to Melbourne since 2007 in addition to meals and a souvenir item; they are also offered free medical care if needed during the tournament. Meanwhile, at Wimbledon ball kids are compensated with meals throughout their stay while they also receive a commemorative pin badge upon completion of their duties. French Open ball kids also receive meals and commemorative merchandise, but it was reported that they received €500 in 2016 for helping out with the event.

Though payment for these services is not particularly high compared to other jobs related to tennis events such as umpires or line judges, ball boys and girls play an important role nonetheless by helping keep the playing surface ready for play. Their contribution allows professional players to reach peak performance during matches—thus providing invaluable support that should not go unrecognized.

Traditions of Tennis

Tennis is a sport that has been around for centuries and has played an important role in many cultures. Throughout its history, tennis has developed an array of unique traditions that have been embraced by players from all walks of life. Here are some of the most popular traditions in tennis around the world:

Bowing to the Royal Box The most enduring and well-known tradition in tennis is the bowing or curtsying to the royal box before starting a match at Wimbledon. This practice has been observed since the tournament was first held at Hampton Court Palace, over 200 years ago. Even today, all players participating in this prestigious event must bow or curtsy before beginning their match on Centre Court as a sign of respect and remembrance of its long history.

This age-old custom has become a widely recognized symbol for Wimbledon and serves to remind all those watching that it is one of the four major tournaments—with records going back as far as 1877! Not only does it represent a significant part of tennis' past but also honors the present-day game with its significance still highly respected throughout the sport today.

So if you're ever lucky enough to attend Wimbledon, make sure to keep an eye out for these special moments between each player and spectator alike—paying homage to one of the oldest traditions in sports!

The Fist Bump

This is one of the most well-known traditions in tennis. The fist bump is exchanged between players after a point is completed as a sign of respect for each other's performance. It can also be used to show camaraderie, especially when playing doubles.

The Call For Quiet

Before serving, many players will call out for quiet from the audience or their opponents so that they may concentrate properly on their shot. This tradition ensures that all players are given an equal chance to compete at their best level.

The Wave Goodbye

Upon completing a match, the winning player will typically wave goodbye to his or her opponent as both a gesture of respect and a way to celebrate their victory. It is a grand tradition often displayed by professional players during tournaments and it's one way of showing how competitive sportsmanship should be conducted.

The Towel Exchange
Players are no longer allowed to hand their towels to ball boys or girls.

Court Etiquette For Spectators
There are certain behaviors spectators should avoid during matches such as inappropriate cheering or conversations while points are still going on even if they are rooting for one particular side. Instead spectators should observe silence unless supported by subtle gestures such as polite clapping while demonstrating good sportsmanship towards both opponents regardless of who wins or loses!

The Grand Salute
At professional tournaments worldwide it's customary for winning players to take part in something called "the Grand Salute" whereupon receiving their trophy they salute either side competing against them along with all four corners of the stadium acknowledging everyone involved in making this momentous occasion happen!

The Trophy Presentations
Regardless, if you're playing singles or doubles; upon completion it's always nice etiquettes from participants to thank umpires for doing such an excellent job officiating matches throughout tournament play before taking center-stage during trophy presentations thereafter!

The Mental Aspect of the Game of Tennis

The mental aspect of playing tennis is a critical component that can often determine the difference between victory and defeat. It requires players to have emotional and mental resilience in order to stay focused and motivated throughout their matches, even when put under pressure.

When playing tennis, it's important to stay composed, both mentally and physically. Additionally, being aware of the situation on the court will help you make better decisions and execute shots more accurately. You should also remember to use the breaks between points so that you don't build up too much tension or fatigue during long rallies.

Another important factor for tennis players is having a positive mindset. This means not only remaining optimistic despite some losses but also learning from each setback and using it as an opportunity to improve. Having a positive attitude can go a long way in helping players stay composed in tense situations and keep their focus on the game at hand. Tennis players must also have strong levels of self-belief if they are going to succeed; believing in yourself can make all the difference when it comes to delivering during crucial moments within matches.

Finally, staying physically fit is essential for any tennis player if they are going to reach their potential on the court. Regular exercise helps maintain endurance levels while allowing you time to practice technique drills outside of match play situations. Keeping your body strong will also reduce the likelihood of suffering injuries during matches due to fatigue or poor technique execution; this allows you to remain focused without worrying about injury-related concerns hindering your performance.

Achieving success at tennis requires more than just physical skill—developing a solid mental approach is key if you want to become a top performer on the court!

I also encourage you to read "The Inner Game of Tennis" by Timothy Gallwey. It is an old book, but it has stood the test of time.

Umpires

Australian Open

The referees for the Australian Open are selected based on their qualifications and experience. They must have obtained a high-level of officiating certification, such as the International Tennis Referees Association (ITRA) or Professional Tennis Referee (PTR) certification. Additionally, they must have at least five years of high-level officiating experience on the international circuit.

The selection process is rigorous and includes a review of referees' past performance, evaluation of their technical knowledge, and assessment of their impartiality and decision-making skills in critical situations. The Australian Open also looks for referees who can demonstrate a good understanding of refereeing mechanics, court positioning, score keeping, and other rules related to tennis.

Prior to being appointed for the event, each referee undergoes an intensive training program which covers topics from player management to signaling communication between courtside personnel. This training ensures that the referees are well-equipped in terms of technical knowledge as well as interpersonal skills when dealing with players and officials during the tournament. Hawk-Eye electronic system is used for line calls.

French Open

The French Open selects umpires who hold or have held a gold badge International Tennis Federation (ITF) rating. Gold badge umpires typically officiate Grand Slam, ATP World Tour and

WTA Tour matches. The list includes only those who hold or have held a gold badge as a chair umpire, and not those who hold or have held a similar badge in refereeing or chief umpiring.

Wimbledon

There are usually 42 chair umpires are assigned each day and they are all members of all members of ABTO (Association of British Tennis Officials). Chair Umpires normally umpire two matches a day, although not necessarily on the same court.

The Chief Umpire is responsible for the organization of all on court officiating at The Championships. His role is to assign, supervise and evaluate all of the officials each day. A custom-made computer system and a team of assistants help this process.

Chair Umpires use tablet computers to score the match, with each point scored being displayed automatically on the scoreboards and wimbledon.com. Wireless net cord machines are used by the Chair Umpire on all courts, and the Hawk-Eye electronic system is used for line calls.

US Open Referees

The selection of referees for the US Open is a rigorous and detailed process that takes into consideration not just a referee's experience, but also their knowledge of the sport and its rules. Referees are typically chosen from a pool of highly qualified individuals who possess an extensive knowledge of the sport, including its regulations and guidelines as set forth by the United States Tennis Association (USTA). The USTA chooses referees based on several criteria, including their experience in officiating tournaments, prior reviews from peers or players, and performance ratings. Additionally, referees must have attained a certain level of certification to be considered for selection.

Once selected, USTA-certified referees receive additional training before the start of each tournament season. This training includes instruction in both rules of play and court procedures. Referees also participate in meetings with umpires and players before each match to ensure all involved parties understand expectations and any particularities related to the game's outcome. Furthermore, throughout matches, referees review video footage to ensure fairness and accuracy as well as enforce penalties when necessary.

In summary, the selection process for referees at the US Open is thorough and comprehensive; only those individuals with a deep understanding of tennis rules and regulations are chosen after undergoing rigorous scrutiny by the USTA. This process ensures that all participants in a match receive fair treatment regardless of their playing level or skill set. Hawk-Eye electronic system is used for line calls.

Final Thought

*Tennis has a Great Future with this
Kind of Feeder System!*

I love the winning, I can take the losing, but most of all I love to play. —BORIS BECKER